VOLUME 2

BUILDING
LIFE

a memoir

ADVANCE PRAISE FOR SYLVIA BAER, *LEARNING LIFE*, AND *BUILDING LIFE*

"When I read Sylvia Baer's intensely personal and profound stories, I am reminded of Aesop's Fables—where good conquers evil or darkness is erased by light. Sylvia's memories become our memories—they recall the sights, the smells and the sensations of distant lands and generations past. Again and again, Sylvia's tales awaken something profound inside of us, producing a smile and even tears of joy."

—Lauren Young, Editor, Digital Special Projects, Reuters

"Sylvia has an amazing memory, and amazing memories. Her detailed stories of the relatives, friends, teachers, and students she has encountered in her 70+ years are truly fascinating."

—Lee Gordon, Voiceover Artist

"When I read an excerpt from Sylvia Baer's book of her fascinating life, I know that I not only will be entertained, but I will feel, and find myself truly caring for her characters. Her revelations and insights into the human life journey keep you intrigued. Every story is like a short film filled with unforgettable characters that keep you keep reading and reading."

—Victoria Papale, Artist,
Ancient Paintings and Artifacts Specialist

"Sylvia Baer has a knack for making people cry. Not painfully ugly crying, but heartfelt 'I was there' crying, 'I feel this too' crying. The first time I read one of her stories, something in it resonated so soundly within me that I felt she had observed one of the most painful parts of my life and then based her story on it. I cried for almost an hour, then returned to her page on Facebook to devour more of her writing. Every single one of her tales reveals more about Sylvia—but also about all of us, her readers. She has a skill with writing, which immediately pulls you into the story, into the situation as if you were there with her in the experiences she describes. And her emotions dance off the page and imbed themselves in your heart. Not only is Sylvia Baer a poet, she's also a wonderful master of words."

—Angela Garry, Author

"Sylvia Baer's writings take you on a life journey, filled with stories of family life in Uruguay, Brazil, and New Jersey. It is the journey to adulthood of a girl who is sensitive and kind, devastatingly smart and curious, smart-alecky and resourceful, and wise beyond her years: an Anne of Green Gables of her place and time. It is an inspiration for lovers of words, writing, teaching and life."

—Susan Krysiak, Media Director, MAC,
Cape May, New Jersey

"Sylvia Baer is equal parts Emily Dickinson, Nora Ephron and Gidget! Through her insightful, engaging narratives, gathered from her immigrant girlhood through half a century of teaching at some of the top colleges in the country, this treasure trove of stories from her life will inspire, make you laugh and sometimes bring tears. She's the mom, grandmother, sister and best friend you wish you had. She wants to help everyone live life better and shows us the way here."

—Celeste McCauley, New York City–based Writer and Editor

"In each story, Sylvia not only creates characters and scenarios that instantly captivate her readers, but she also somehow manages to capture in words exactly what it is to be human."

—Dr. Andrea Vinci, Professor of English

VOLUME 2

BUILDING LIFE

a memoir

SYLVIA BAER

Cover design by Semnitz.
Typesetting by Susan Gerber.

For media inquiries, questions about bulk purchases, permission to use any of the content of this book, or speaking availability, please visit www.sylviabaerwrites.com.

Library of Congress CIP is on file.

ISBN 979-8-9864361-3-5 (hardcover)
ISBN 979-8-9864361-4-2 (paperback)
ISBN 979-8-9864361-5-9 (ebook)

This book is dedicated to John Baer,
"for the longest time"

CONTENTS

GENERATION TO GENERATION
–Antoine de Saint-Exupéry

In a house which becomes a home,
one hands down and another takes up
the heritage of mind and heart,
laughter and tears, musings and deeds.
Love, like a carefully loaded ship,
crosses the gulf between the generations.
Therefore, we do not neglect the ceremonies
of our passage: when we wed, when we die,
and when we are blessed with a child;
When we depart and when we return;
When we plant and when we harvest.
Let us bring up our children. It is not
the place of some official to hand to them
their heritage.
If others impart to our children our knowledge
and ideals, they will lose all of us that is
wordless and full of wonder.
Let us build memories in our children,
lest they drag out joyless lives,
lest they allow treasures to be lost because
they have not been given the keys.
We live, not by things, but by the meanings
of things. It is needful to transmit the passwords
from generation to generation.

PREFACE

Walt Whitman wrote a poem about a spider tossing threads ("filaments") out of itself, hoping they might land somewhere hospitable so it can begin to build a web. As do I, he connects this idea to himself:

> Ceaselessly musing, venturing, throwing, seeking the
>   spheres to connect them,
> Till the bridge you will need be form'd, till the ductile
>   anchor hold,
> Till the gossamer thread you fling catch somewhere,
>   O my soul.

None of us exists in a vacuum—we are all intertwined with each other and with our own pasts in ways we can't often see. Our awareness of these connections comes briefly and sometimes without warning. Just such moments happen to me in my most fortunate hours, and I race to jot them down haphazardly, hoping that one day I can write them more clearly—and hoping too that when I send them out into the world, these experiences and memories can connect to others.

Right now, dear reader, you are holding my latest attempt. I hope that my stories bring you moments of illumination into your own life and remind you of times you too felt or thought or acted as I did.

Thank you for joining me in this journey of building my life. Although the names of non-family members in this book have been changed out of respect for their privacy, all the events and encounters herein are true—with small bits of color tossed in here and there.

May your kind eyes find connections in these threads.

"I dwell in Possibility"

–Emily Dickinson

CHAPTER 1
GENERATION

I could not stop crying. The hard wooden pew I was sitting in seemed unyielding and protecting at the same time. I put my left hand on the creviced wood. On my right, my husband took a big white handkerchief out of his suit pocket and nudged it into my hands. Like a surrender flag, it dangled from my fingers.

His aunt Hannah had died, and the funeral that day in May 1999 was in a family Mennonite church. Hannah was born in 1905—one of many children—at the family farm in Hagerstown, Maryland. By the time I met her in 1998 I had heard a few minor stories of her life. Her brother, my father-in-law, had recently arranged for her to relocate from Kansas to a nursing facility near their childhood home. I visited her there a few times.

On the first visit I didn't know what to expect. The halls smelled of disinfectant and my shoes clanged on the linoleum as I walked toward her room. I wanted to carry something welcoming to her and wasn't sure what sort of thing I might offer. That morning I finally settled on my favorite: a bunch of sunflowers. They were awkward in my arms as I opened her door.

"Oh my lands!" she squealed, using a typical Maryland expression—a bright smile lighting up her porcelain face—when I walked in. "Those are my favorites!" She got up from a brown-striped easy chair, slowly but effectively steadying herself. Quickly and efficiently she cut the thick green stems to fit the happy bouquet into a nearby white ironware pitcher. "Don't they just brighten everything up, Sylvia?" She beamed and continued, "They are such sturdy plants—and so useful." She sighed as her wrinkled and arthritis-gnarled fingers touched the gold petals, the rough seed-filled centers.

We were both startled when a few hours later a nurse came in with her afternoon medicines. As she swallowed and sipped, I looked out of her west-facing window and watched the sun slowly sliding earthward. "I better get home, Aunt Hannah," I stammered. "It's getting late."

She smiled. "'Deed it is, my girl. 'Deed it is. You be safe on the roads now, hear?" I hugged her and left.

I visited her one more time and once again with an armful of our favorite flower. She had grown much more frail in the past few weeks. This time I was the one to cut the hard stems, fill the pitcher with water, and place the display next to her bed. She could not move, and the monitor at her side, on the edge of the bed, made a soft whirring noise.

"You know," she said in almost a whisper, "my nephew, your husband, is a very smart man. He went to Yale." I nodded and she continued, "But I was the first Baer to go there." I didn't understand. Yale didn't admit women until 1969—my own sophomore year of college. "It was the nursing school," she said with a wink, "and I got my master's degree there."

She told me about nursing and about her life setting up health programs in her town and about moving to Kansas where she lived with her second husband until his death several years earlier. And more.

As she slowly closed her eyes and took a few shallow breaths, I looked around her small room. There, on the counter by her sink, was a luminous painting I had not seen before. "Hannah," I asked when she opened her eyes and smiled at me, "where did that come from? It's beautiful." She had created it. It was her own work. And then she told me of her life as an artist—her love of color and movement and the power of creating images on surfaces that seemed empty and lonely.

She continued, "And I especially love our favorite flower. You know that it's beautiful when it's young with its face mirroring the warmth of the sun. But after it gets more mature, its roots help to nourish and cleanse the soil it's in. Actually heals it. Amazing." To still a small, persistent cough, she took a sip of the water I handed her and then continued. "After it's finished its active life—after its color is gone—after it can't help the earth in the old way anymore, then the seeds are ready.

The seeds from the dying plant feed the birds and the critters, can get pressed into oil for cooking, and can be nibbled on by people. And some seeds fall back to the ground and grow into new flowers."

Her coughing was getting worse. I called for the nurse, who brought soothing syrup. "I better go, Hannah," I said reluctantly, "you need to rest." She nodded, but suddenly opened her eyes. "That painting," she said motioning with her head, "I asked them to bring that from storage this morning. I want you to have it. I want it to have a new life in your home. I want . . . I want it to be useful in the world."

I hugged her delightedly, holding her almost fleshless body in my arms.

The following week she died.

But look! Now. Here is the painting on my wall. The brilliant sturdy flower heads—the green stems and leaves—shining on the slate background. These sunflowers are miraculous and resilient in their many forms. Like Hannah. Like so many others.

Sometimes, like me.

CHAPTER 2

MARIA ELENA

"You're my favorite teacher in the whole world. I'm going to miss you a lot," Maria Elena told me as we both realized I would be moving very far away in a few weeks. It was 1956 and we were both six years old and in the first grade at Crandon Institute in Montevideo, Uruguay.

I giggled and said, "I'm not a teacher. I'm in your same grade." But in truth, I had been working with her for over a month. Maria Elena had recovered from polio, but the disease had left her with a serious limp and a drooping left arm.

When she came back to school some kids made fun of her. They passed notes about how she walked like a monster. Señora Riaz intercepted some of those and tried to quiet the gossip, but was unsuccessful. On a Tuesday morning during arithmetic, I looked over and saw Maria Elena, head bent down, quietly crying and trying to wipe away tears with her awkward left hand. Jose Alvarez started an ugly chant about her which the kids took up. The teacher tried to quiet them down but was not very successful.

I had had enough. I stood up and with all of my six-year-old fury banged my fist on my wooden desk and yelled as loudly as I could: "Stop this minute. Stop. Stop. Stop." A very startled group of kids suddenly quieted down and stared at me. I continued, "It's stupid stupid stupid to make fun of someone else. You should all be embarrassed."

I didn't wait. I marched out of the room and walked myself to the principal's office where I felt sure Señora Riaz would send me. I told my story to the principal, Señor Hernandez, said I was ready for my punishment, but I was not sorry for what I did.

"Well, Sylvia, you can't yell every day. That's not right." I nodded in agreement and he continued, "How do you think we can fix the real problem here?"

I was surprised. He was asking my opinion. I was eager to speak up. "Señor Hernandez, I think there are two big problems. One is that people don't understand when others aren't just like them. It's like they're scared and angry because they don't understand. And the other problem is that Maria Elena is going to take a long time to do some stuff she used to love to do and it's going to make her sad."

He nodded, and I continued, "I can't do much about the first problem. But I can help Maria Elena with jump rope. That's her favorite and my favorite too."

He sent me back to class with a note for the teacher. When I walked into the room everyone was silent. I gave the note to

Señora Riaz, took my seat, and looked over at a shyly smiling Maria Elena. By recess everyone had forgotten the incident, but the playground director came over to me and showed me a special spot away from everyone where Maria Elena and I could practice jump rope.

For the next month practice was just what we did. I'd go home at night and think of ways to make it easier—step by step. I drew little charts and wrote notes on the progress. I tried using chalk on the black asphalt to mark off where the rope should hit each revolution. When she fell, I helped her up at first and then she figured out how to do it herself.

And then she could jump. At first by using one foot then the other—steplike. But then (Oh joy!) both feet together. Up then down quickly while controlling the rotation of the rope, over and under her body.

By the end of the school term she was ready. We went out to the full playground and together began jumping rope. At first some kids pointed, others laughed nervously. But that didn't stop us. Soon others began jumping rope and the boys who had been such bullies ignored us and went about their own games pushing and shoving each other down.

Marta, a second grader, came over to us and asked if we wanted to play with her and some of her friends. Susana told us her brother had polio and couldn't walk at all. Marcela's sister had it and was in a big machine that helped her breathe. Teresa showed us a new game using string and your own fingers. And by the end of recess we were all laughing and talking and singing little songs together.

Señor Hernandez stopped me on our way back into the

building and asked to see me in his office. "Sylvia, I see that you've worked very hard with your friend. She's made good progress. And now I will try very hard to make progress with the first problem you talked about. But that will take a lot of time and I don't know if I can make that happen. How hard it is to show people how to be kind to each other. To respect each other." He sighed, looked out the window and then at his wall to a photograph of some men in uniform all standing at attention. We knew he had fought in the war, but no one dared ever talk about it.

Then he continued, "But here's what I do know: I will do everything I can, but when you're ready, you too can help. You see, you are a born teacher. Not just because you teach how to do something, but because you want to help people be better. You can make a difference no matter where you are in the world. One person at a time." I nodded and grinned widely, remembering that in a few short weeks my family and I would be moving very far away to the United States.

"I will do my very best, Señor Hernandez," I vowed, and walked back to my classroom ready for the next chapter to begin.

CHAPTER 3

OTRA VEZ

"Otra vez, otra vez (again, again)!" I shouted with glee. It was 1956, I was six years old, and doing one of my favorite things of the week: listening to Señora Maria Jose tell stories. She came to our home in Carrasco (a suburb of Montevideo, Uruguay) once a week to do our ironing. At that time, in that place, it was not uncommon to have, as we did, a cook (Señora Marcela), a housekeeper (Señora Mariana), and a laundry helper (Señora Maria Jose).

Every Thursday Señora Maria Jose would come to our home and iron a week's worth of linens. She was very precise and took great pride in her sharp creases and impeccably folded corners. I marveled at the magic of taking a crumpled-up piece of white cloth and turning it into a pristine rectangle. Like a perfect piece of papel (paper), I would declare. She would shake her head and laugh. "Ah, Sylvita, you and your pieces of paper!" Then Señora Marcela would chime in with a stern tone which I knew to be false, "She has papers and books all over her tiny room. It's like a messy library in there. And she won't let me throw anything away! Niña, what are we going to do with you?"

As was the custom, children ate in the kitchen with the workers on weeknights, and I couldn't be happier about this arrangement. This meant that I could hear all sorts of stories of the day from the small band of women. And on Thursdays, Señora Maria Jose would be a treasure trove of tales. Sometimes she would regale us with the goings-on in her small town (two bus rides away), and sometimes, like today, she would tell stories of growing up.

"Yes, Miguel was in very big trouble that day," she began an often-told story. "He was only one year younger than I was and always pulling pranks on everyone. That was the day—I think it was back in 1910 when he was nine and I was ten—that he brought a giant frog into the house and put it in Mama's special cooking pot. When she opened it and the green creature jumped out at her, we thought she was going to have a heart attack. But she grabbed the biggest wooden spoon she had and started chasing Miguel all over the yard until she was too tired to continue. He had to hide in the little barn all night long."

The vivid descriptions of the scene sent all of us into peals of laughter. "Was Miguel one of the kids that lived?" I asked, knowing from previous stories that she had eleven brothers and sisters, but only three lived into adulthood.

"No, Sylvita, he did not. He died a few years later," she

answered sighing. And then Señora Marcela ladled up an extra helping of her delicious chicken soup for each of us and I listened contentedly while they gossiped and chatted amiably.

The next Thursday Señora Maria Jose did not come. "A tragedy," I overheard my mother say on the phone. And then the women of the neighborhood who also used her ironing services were in our living room. I was banished to my room, and try as I might I could only hear small snatches of the story. "What will she do?" "Is he able to move at all?" "They won't have enough food." "What about all the bills?" "She has no children to come help out." "She won't let anyone give her anything. Too proud." Try as I might, I was given no more information.

But to my great joy, Señora Maria Jose came twice the next week. She did not want to talk about what happened when I was in the room, but when I was banished to my nighttime bath and then bed, she uncharacteristically stayed in the kitchen with the other two women. This went on for many months.

I woke up once to get a glass of water and found them huddled together at the kitchen table. My mother was pouring tea for them and when she saw me, she got me the water and rushed me off to bed.

When I found out that we would be moving to the United States I knew it would be a long time before I saw any of them again. "It will be a brand-new start for us," my father said. "We will be very happy there," my mother said. I was excited for the adventure and wanted to give them each a present to remember me by. I had no money but what I had was paper and pencils. I wrote each one a special goodbye note and on our last night together, while they were busy in the kitchen as my parents threw a large final party for all of our friends, I ceremoniously handed a folded paper to the three of them. They each read my words and softly glanced at Señora Maria Jose, who was crying. "This is the most beautiful present I ever received," she gushed while hugging me close.

The next day I told my parents how excited and moved by my words Señora Maria Jose had been. They smiled and looked strangely at each other.

About ten years later one of my parents' friends from Carrasco, Señora Velazco, came to visit us in New York. I listened through a long dinner of catching up with the events that had unfolded and families that had moved or broken apart since we had left. Scandals and loves and deaths. As the last cup of coffee was being served, she turned to me and said, "Oh, you should know that Señora Maria Jose still has that note you gave her before you left. She reads it often." I smiled fondly at the memory. My mother chimed in, "So, things worked out for her?" I was confused. I needed information.

And so they told me: Señora Maria Jose had come from a dirt poor neighborhood. Her family often went hungry and two of her sisters had died from malnutrition as babies. She had never been to school and to help feed her family she had worked many hours every day taking in laundry from the time she was about five years old. When she married, her husband built them a house with the luxury of an indoor toilet, and she felt like a queen. Her ironing skills were legendary and she was able to make enough money to supplement her husband's small wages as a factory worker.

But on that day in 1956, the tragedy happened: her husband had a massive stroke which left him paralyzed. She was now the only support for them. And she could neither read nor write.

What was happening right there in our kitchen and in kitchens throughout our community was the education of Señora Maria Jose. The cooks and the housekeepers who were literate banded together to help her learn so that she could understand her husband's medical care, and the household bills, and the information that came in envelopes daily. And all the women who hired her made sure to give her an extra amount of work, even when it was not strictly needed, so she could spend extra time learning.

And then my mother told me, "The goodbye note you gave her was the first time she realized she could read. She could read it all the way through." I was speechless. "And," my parents' friend continued, "she said that you would always be her favorite writer."

My father shook his head with admiration and said, "It seems that when people band together to do something good—to smooth out problems—the results can be . . ." He stumbled for the word, and then, "Magical. Just magical."

CHAPTER 4

TONTA

"Sara, of course she's going to fall. She has to learn that what's important is getting up. She will fall time and time again. I'm with her right now. She's capable. She has to learn so that when we're not at her side and she falls, she'll know how to get back up."

My father was teaching me to ride a bike. It was 1956, I was six years old, and we were living in Montevideo, Uruguay. I had watched the older kids riding down the street and it looked so powerfully graceful and free that I was determined to learn. My father was happy to help and even bought me a bicycle. "Look, Sara," he said to my fretting mother, "it has training wheels. She'll be on these until she gets the hang of it."

This was new territory for my mom. She had always been a worrier and most of the childish risks I had taken—climbing that tree in the yard, balancing on a pogo stick around three blocks, bouncing basketballs where the big kids hung out—I kept from her. But this—this was happening before her very eyes.

After several days I had mastered the training wheels, and I was ready. My father very ceremoniously took off the extra support and as I climbed onto the seat he instructed me. "Sylvia, you need to get a little speed to stay upright. Put your weight like this in the middle. Keep your eyes ahead of you. Feel the power of the metal guiding you forward." And first holding onto the seat-back while running behind me, then letting go, he watched me navigate my first foray into my own power. My mother went inside the house, unable to watch. It was all gloriously liberating.

And then I fell.

My dad ran over to me, took his handkerchief to my bleeding left knee, and assessed the situation. "Well, that was a good fall. What do you want to do now?" he asked. I hesitated, crumpled on the ground, my bike a heap beside me, and he continued, "The way I see it you can stop and try again another day, you can stop right now and give up the bike, or you can take a deep breath and try again right now. What would you like to do?" He seemed to have no preference, leaving the decision completely up to me. I thought hard about this and decided I needed to try again right then and there. After two more falls, I was fine. I glided and soared around the block away from my house, away from my yard, away from my waiting father.

Afterwards he hugged me. "Remember this ride forever,

OK? Remember that you fell and got up and fell again and got up again. We have to learn how to fall in life so we can know the power in getting up." I assured him I would write that down in my little notebook, but right then I wanted to ride to my friend Mariana's house to show her my new skill.

Mariana lived two blocks away and was my best friend in school. Her father died when she was little and her mother always seemed to be worried or crying. Her older brother, Geraldo, was terribly mean to us and to everyone. Today when I got to her house Geraldo and his friends were watching something on TV. Television was new in the world and I had never seen it. "Wow, look at that," I exclaimed as I walked into their living room. "How does that happen right here in your house?" Without skipping a beat, Geraldo said that there were tiny men inside the big box and that's what we were seeing. I believed him.

And then he and all of his fourth-grade friends laughed cruelly. "Tonta (stupid)," they yelled, pointing at me. Then rhythmically, "Tonta, tonta, tonta." Mariana pulled me away to her front yard before I could burst into tears. And with blurry, water-filled eyes, I found my way home, where I parked my bike and collapsed on the front lawn.

My dad came out and between sobs I told him of my humiliation. "Well, that was terrible. You must have felt horrible. Those boys were mean." I nodded violently in agreement, and he continued, "But now you have a choice. Their words may have made your heart bleed—like falling off the bike hurt your knee—but there will be a scab, and then you'll be fine. Or you can just be afraid forever." He hugged me. "This won't be the last time. But you have the power to get back up. Power is not lost in falling—it's lost in not getting back up."

A few days later I rode my bike the three blocks to the empty basketball court. As I neared it, I saw Geraldo with a bike. I watched from a safe distance and realized he didn't know how to ride. He seemed afraid and he was trying to teach himself. Suddenly he looked up and saw me. "Che, tonta," he yelled at me. But there was no sting in his words. "What are you looking at?"

And from somewhere inside I found the strength to answer. "I'm looking at someone who could use my help learning how to ride." At first he refused, but I persisted and we began. It didn't take too long. He was really quite athletic and talented. "The key is," I said, "that when you fall, you know you can get right back up. That's real power." I left him to practice and went home.

A few weeks later I was in a school show. As a first grader I had qualms about getting up in front of the whole school and saying my lines. The big kids would all be there and they might laugh at little me in a cat costume running down the aisle, onto the stage, and reciting a long poem. But I had been the one chosen out of my entire grade and I had written my dad's words down in my little notebook and read them to myself right before the performance.

I played my part and when I was finished I heard a yell from the audience. Geraldo had stood up tall and was yelling "Bravo" loud and clear. Then his friends joined in and pretty soon the rest of the school. I smiled, took a dramatic bow, and went off-stage.

Afterwards my parents met me by the school's side door. "That was a fine performance," my dad said. "You looked so cute," my mom said. Geraldo saw me. "Che, tonta," he said with warmth and a smile, "you're a powerful little kid."

Learn that falling down just gives you the opportunity to practice your power of getting back up. That's what I had in my notebook and what I've read hundreds and hundreds of times throughout my long life.

CHAPTER 5

YOU MUST BE VERY QUIET

"You must be very quiet today, Sylvinka, we have a visitor who needs peace."

It was 1956, I was six years old, and visiting my Meindl grandparents as I did by myself every Sunday. They lived several blocks away from us in Montevideo, Uruguay, but going to see them always felt to me like being in a whole different world. Pieces of their former lives in Prague embraced their small apartment. Some rescued teacups, small paintings, an old worn doll, bits of intricate lace doilies, a rough-edged scrap of tapestry gently layered on the wooden dining table.

And their language. The Czech language, and sometimes German, that they spoke to each other sounded guttural and strange to my Spanish-accustomed ears. I loved the play of it when my grandfather would show me words with symbols and letters that looked like they were dancing across a page. After he translated them into Spanish I would giggle at the wonder of such different-looking words having the same meanings in another language. "Ah, Sylvinka," he would say, using my Czech name, "you see, the whole world is connected even when it looks so different on the page."

So on this day when he admonished me to be very quiet, I was curious. To my surprise there was a man sitting in their dark blue living room chair, staring out the window. He was slumped to one side and looked more like a large hamper of crumpled dirty laundry than a man. He stood up as he heard me walk in and then turned to greet me, holding onto the side of the furniture for support.

My grandfather introduced us. "Sylvinka, this is Jozsef. He will be staying with us for a little while. He has recently come from Hungary." I smiled and curtsied as I had been trained to do in greeting adults. He stared at me with his piercing blue eyes, mumbled vague words, smiled faintly, and slipped off to the guest room.

My grandfather sat me down to explain the situation as best he could to six-year-old me. "You know that we came to this country because of the war in Europe. We had to flee quickly in order to save our lives. But war and oppression did not stop. First one country then another took over our lands." He stood up to get something from the top drawer of a nearby cabinet. I had never seen him look angry before, but now he tightened his jaw as he showed me the round gold coin that he held. "Do you see this? It is from the Austro-Hungarian nation I was born in. But after the First World War, in 1918, the country was changed by others into a new one—Czechoslovakia.

And then again it was taken over in 1939, and then again in 1948." He wrote those dates down for me, his angry hand making the penciled numbers dark and thick.

And he continued, "And now, there is trouble again. Young Jozsef has come here seeking asylum. He does not want to be killed and we will shelter him."

This was very confusing to me. But I had no time right then to ask questions because my grandmother called us to dinner. Jozsef came into the dining room, sat down tentatively at the table, looked around anxiously, and began to weep openly. He stood quickly—knocking over his chair—and retreated to his room.

No one spoke. My grandmother filled a plate—a dish from her prized Herend china, with birds painted in the middle and along the edges, which came out only for special occasions—with food and carried it back to him.

My grandfather explained, "You see, Jozsef is considered dangerous to the new powers in the country. They have tried to kill him. They have killed many of his friends."

My eager and vivid mind was quick to imagine terrible things this man must have done. Terrible atrocities. But I could not reconcile that with my grandparents harboring such a criminal. And so I asked, "Why then do you have him here? What terrible things did he do?"

My grandfather let out a strange laugh and responded, "He is a poet. A poet."

I was astounded. "But you are a poet, Abuelo, and I write poetry too. How can that be so dangerous?"

He looked at me with sad, troubled eyes and answered,

"Words are powerful. Sometimes they are more powerful than even guns or tanks or bombs. Those destructive things can kill people and destroy villages and cities. But words have wings and travel. They begin to live in the hearts of people all over the world. You can destroy a lot of things, but words have a different kind of life."

I was not sure I fully understood what he was conveying to me. But over the next few months, I saw Jozsef writing and growing stronger. My grandparents had found him new clothing and supplied him with paper and ink and envelopes. Every week I saw a stack of mail to go out in Monday's post sitting in the front entry.

In October, he was gone as mysteriously as he appeared. "Where will he live now?" I asked anxiously.

"Well," my grandfather replied, "he has found refuge in America. He will go there to live. He was hired to write for a big magazine there and a newspaper. You see, Sylvinka, words are very powerful instruments. This is why they are feared. And why they are necessary. Some day in the far future"—now he paused as his lower lip trembled and he took a deep breath—"in the far future, you can be a writer. You can tell stories of people and their lives. This is how the world understands and how the world—all the world—heals."

When my own family left for the United States several months later, my grandmother gave me the one childhood memento she had from long ago Prague—from the very beginning of the twentieth century. As she placed it in my hands she said, "Para tener presente" (to remember—to keep present). And my grandfather said, "Write this story. It will have wings."

CHAPTER 6

BIRTH

"So, Abuela, is this the real date?" My grandmother and I were going through some scattered bits of paper in her dresser drawer. It was 1957, I was seven years old and getting ready to move to the United States with my mother and father. My grandmother was anxious. She wanted to make sure her own documents were up to date so she could visit us in the future, and was searching for her passport.

"Ah, Sylvia, my clever girl, you found it!" she exclaimed, quickly taking the small notebook-like object from my hands. My grandmother never celebrated her birthday and we actually didn't know the day. Or the year. But I had just spied it on her document: December 31, 1899.

She sat me down and showed me some of the pages in the passport. Stamps with strange-looking letters and numbers, places I could not pronounce, and her picture, a profile, the only unflattering one of her I had ever seen.

"You see, my girl, that was not really my birthday," she began with a sly grin and a wink of her left eye, her dimples like small parentheses around her mouth. "I decided to give myself that birthday."

Now I was intrigued. My grandmother could make anything happen—this fact had been true her whole life. So it wasn't surprising to me that she could just conjure up a birthdate. "But why that day, Abuela? What was special about it?" I asked.

"Well, when I left Poland in such a hurry with your mother, who was your age—seven—and your uncle, who was three years younger, we didn't have our real documents. Those had been taken from us to try to keep us from escaping to safety. Hitler's army did not want us to live. So, I hired someone to make official documents for us. I paid him money that I had hidden away in my teapot. Oh, it was a lot that I had saved."

Now she paused and looked down at that little book again and continued. "The man asked me what my birthday was. It was a normal question but I decided to make my answer different."

"You lied?" I exclaimed, my eyes fairly jumping out of my face.

"Well, yes I did," she continued, "but in a sense it was true. I wanted to have a brand-new life with my children— one where we didn't worry so much about people trying to hurt us. We were going to a faraway country with a whole new language. Everything was going to be new. So I thought hard about my answer."

I was still confused about her choice, so she explained. "December 31st is the very end of the year. 1899 is the very end of the whole century. I wanted my birthday to be just when everything old is like a warm comfortable blanket I wrap around me as I walk into the place where everything is about to be brand new. Like my life."

Just then my mother came rushing into the room directing me to finish getting ready for bed. As I hugged her good-night I asked her what her real birthday was and she replied, "December 31st, 1899, because that date brought me here, with you."

We never knew the day my grandmother was physically born, or the year. But each December 31st I pull the old year tightly around me for warmth and look up at the stars eager for the life awaiting me in the new year. And I celebrate her life and mine and the lives of all the people on earth that ever have been or ever will be.

CHAPTER 7

A STUDENT STORY: WILLIAM

It was April 1998. He came into my college office on a Monday afternoon during office hours looking more disheveled than usual. I had gotten used to his dirt-covered overalls and torn-up sneakers. But today he looked weary. "Oh my—what have you got there?" I asked, nodding toward the large cardboard box he gently placed on my empty conference table. He grinned. It was good to see him smile again.

We were near the end of his fourth semester in one of my classes. Last year his third semester was a rough one. Although I had seen his eagerness to read and respond to literature, his many absences were a problem. By the middle of that semester we both knew he was failing and at my request he stayed after class to talk with me about this.

"I don't know what to do, Dr. Baer. My mother's been threatening to throw me out of the house if I don't change. I tried. Really I did. But I'm just who I am and I can't seem to be different. I'm just . . . just . . ." He looked up at the ceiling almost in supplication to the sky, sighed, and continued. "I'm just sinful. I'm a sinner. My folks told me this when they found me kissing Bob in September."

He looked at me almost in horror, realizing he had blurted something out meant to be hidden. I nodded sympathetically. He continued, "My dad tried to whip the sin out of me and my mom made me pray for hours every day. They wanted to send me away to some sort of camp to get this sin out of me. But I begged and pleaded not to go. So I tried to change."

His head hung down as he stared at his feet. And he continued, "You know that Dickinson poem about where they tried to make her one way but she just couldn't be that? That's me."

Ah yes. Dickinson had proven to be his favorite that semester. Before that it was *Wuthering Heights*. Before that it was all of Shakespeare's sonnets. I jumped in, "Do you mean the one where she says, 'They shut me up in Prose—//As when a little Girl—//They put me in the Closet—//Because they liked me "still"—'?"

"Yes," he exclaimed, "that's the one. I love that one as much as all the garden and flower ones."

William had a dream of owning his own greenhouse one day. He seemed to know everything about growing things and his essays and poetry were full of botanical references and metaphors. He was able to pay for his tuition by working at a local garden center stocking shelves and hauling heavy items for customers. "Just knowing that folks are taking those plants home and caring for them and giving them what they need— well, it makes me happy," he'd tell me.

At our mid-semester conference, after hearing about his situation, I referred him to a college counselor (although there were still very few services at the time), and I decided on an alternative route to his studies. I found other ways for him to demonstrate his literary knowledge and, already knowing his skill for writing, I let him explore his expression in a variety of ways. At semester's end he presented me with his final project: an herbarium, based on one that Emily Dickinson had created in the 1800s but this one had his writings among his pressed leaves and flower parts. The magnificent beauty of each page almost took my breath away.

But now, this April 1998, he looked beaten down as he sat wearily at the round conference table. "After my parents kicked me out last year I've been living with my grandmom. Been taking care of her and she let me plant my flowers in her little yard. But she thinks I'm a sinner also. Wants me to ask forgiveness every day." He sighed. I talked with him for a good while, gave him numbers to call for help and support, and reassured him as best I could.

And then he opened the box sitting between us. "These are dahlias, Dr. Baer. They're mine. I got them a couple of years ago for almost nothing from the garden center's leftover pile. I wrote out the instructions for how to plant them and take care of them. I won't have a garden space soon, so I want to think of them being taken care of. I want you to have them.

They won't last too long, but when you see them bloom . . . well, it's amazing. It's like that Dickinson poem about all the things a flower has to overcome just to bloom."

He took one of the strange-looking twisted and gnarled tubers out of the box and explained the life cycle to me. I was delighted to have this box full of potential. As he left my office he slowly turned to say goodbye and grabbed my hand in both of his. Tears were spilling down his face. "I'll see you in class next week!" I said—confused by the intensity of his farewell. "But call my office if you need something, OK?"

He left.

That weekend I set out the tubers and readied them for planting in my garden. Lined them up neatly one by one. Dug holes just deep enough to tuck them into the soft, nutritious soil. And gave them a long drink of water.

On Monday William was not in class. The department dean informed me that afternoon that William was found dead on Saturday evening, and that no one knew what to make of the last lines of the short note he had written and was left next to where they found his body. And then as I sat there weeping, the dean read the lines which I knew to be the very end of Walt Whitman's great poem "Song of Myself" from *Leaves of Grass*, a favorite of William's, " 'I bequeath myself to the dirt to grow from the grass I love,//If you want me again look for me under your bootsoles.' "

Today, once again, I planted dahlias.

CHAPTER 8

A ROSEMARY

"What's that one called? I need to write it down."

It was January 1957. I was a few days shy of my seventh birthday and the next week we were going to make the big move from where I'd always lived, Montevideo, Uruguay, to my father's country and language, the United States and English. I was following our gardener, Señor Jose Felipe, around the back garden. I loved the stories he would tell me about each of the plants—the mimosa that was so timid that if you touched the leaves it would coyly turn itself inward. Or the rosemary with its powerful headlong acceptance of all sorts of trials and tribulations of seaside air and storms only to emerge resilient and wonderfully fragrant. And the verbena with its extravagantly purple flowers waving greetings to all who stopped by to visit.

Señor Jose Felipe was old. He had told me that once we

left, he was going to retire. "I love my plants, but my back and knees are rebelling against me," he would chuckle. "I'll stay in my shack near the beach and watch the water and drink maté. It's a good life. Look at all the beauty it gives us, ah, Sylvia," he'd say, leaning on his rake and spreading his right arm as if to cover the land around us.

On this day, before he left, he gave me a small coin. I had no idea then the sacrifice he made to give me this, but I recognized the power of it. "Keep this with you. For emergencies." He patted my shoulder.

That coin traveled with me in the right-hand pocket of my blue coat. I reached down to hold it between my fingers on the tumultuous plane trip north, when we landed in Texas, and as we began our car trip across to California. I held it and felt its slightly raised outlines and ridged edges as we traveled up the rocky coast, stopping in one city and then another and staying at small cramped motels while my father went to interviews for jobs. "I think San Francisco is next," he told us one day. "I think that's where we might have a chance."

My mother was always anxious and when they thought I was asleep on one of the roll-away cots I slept on, I could hear her crying and him trying to reassure her. In San Francisco it was no different. But something in my mother began to change. Instead of watching television most of the day—how we were both just beginning to learn English—she took us on a bus ride around the city. It was thrilling. The words from strangers' mouths flew around my ears and once in a while I'd catch one in recognition. "Soap," and "water," and "children" began to have some meaning to me now.

I had run out of room in the one little notebook I was allowed to take with me from Uruguay, so I wrote down what I could on my leftover paper napkins. But they tore so easily and it was hard to keep them in order in my small suitcase. Asking for new notebooks was out of the question—we had so little right now and the constant and many worries about money hung on our bodies and in our car and in the very air we breathed.

So, our bus trip around town was a delight. We finally stopped at a garden that was the most glorious place I had ever seen. A giant glass building with rows and rows and circles and towers of brilliantly hued flowers. Oh, how Señor Jose Felipe would have loved this. I wanted to write to him and to describe everything. I made pictures in my mind hoping that someday soon I could write them down. The yellows and blues and that spiky orange flower and something called a gardenia. A gardenia that smelled like . . .

I had always been able to describe what things looked like, but not smells. Smells seemed to me beyond the reach of the words I had. But there, in that glass house, I found the words for the scent. I never wanted to forget that.

My mother and I wandered around by bus and by foot for most of the afternoon. Finally, we came to a big store on a corner with books piled up in the window. At first I thought it was a library, but my mother could read the name. " 'Bookstore'—tienda," she told me. "They sell books. But you can't buy anything. No money." I nodded, but it was books. I wanted to go see them. She didn't, so she sat outside on a nearby bench while I ventured in.

It was like I was imagining this in a strange flowing dream. The smoke was thick. Grown men and women were sitting on the floor in a circle, cross-legged, reading aloud, many with eyes closed nodding to the words almost in prayer. It was another world. I walked around touching the books in awe.

And then I saw it. A notebook on the counter. With a price tag. A notebook. I thought Señor Jose Felipe would agree that this was an emergency. I had to write everything down. I could wait no longer. I held his coin between my fingers, my palm sweating, and finally clinked it onto the counter. The woman by the register spoke to me in English and I did not understand. She pushed the coin away saying a word I did comprehend, "No." I tried to explain but in a language that was foreign to her. I was in despair.

A kind man who had been in the circle on the floor stood up and came over to me. His eyes looked sad behind the thick lenses of his glasses. His bearded face tilted to one side comfortingly as he began to speak to me in Spanish. I was so grateful for the familiarity of a common language between us. In a rush, I explained about our travels and my need to write but napkins being inadequate and how I came to have my emergency coin and why I need a notebook right now because I finally had the words to describe the most delicious flower smell in the whole world.

"Well," he said, "it seems quite important and I do understand. But we don't sell things to children here. Hmmm. . . . How old are you?"

"Seven," I said, "last month I turned seven."

"Ah, well, now I understand. You see, for children of that age we don't sell notebooks; we give them in exchange for a story. Now you told me a story, so here," he said, taking the notebook from the counter and placing it in my left hand and the coin in my right, "you write for the rest of your life. Live life and write life. Can I give you a word for your book? A word—maybe a few—in English?" I smiled delightedly and handed it to him.

Before he wrote in large letters on the first page, he asked, "So, how do you describe that smell?" I told him, "It smelled like the big shiny moon sparkling on a calm sea making a whole line of dancing stars on the water."

He sighed and grinned, translated what I had said in Spanish into English to the cross-legged group and they clapped and snapped fingers appreciatively. I giggled and bowed.

I put the notebook in my pocket, went outside to my waiting mother, and we reluctantly went back to the motel.

Our travels east—"toward our waiting future" as my father called it—took several weeks more. I never needed to spend Señor Jose Felipe's coin given to me in kindness and for memory. And I kept my notebook—a gift given to me for a story.

Later I understood the words on that first page, in big letters that the kind bespectacled man had written: "Keep finding wonder. It's all around us. And then show the world. Write it."

CHAPTER 9

MUTABILITY

When we landed in Dallas, Texas, from Montevideo, Uruguay, in 1957, my seven-year-old self gazed around. I held my face up to the sky, spread my arms wide, and with dramatic flair said (in Spanish—the only language I knew), "This is my new home."

As we drove from Texas to California and from California to New York in a series of job searches and interviews for my (American) father, I reveled in the sights and sounds and landscapes of my new country. "Mama, look!" I would yell, trying to direct her attention to the wonders outside our windows as our black 1951 Buick inched its way up one side and then down the other of the Sierra Nevada mountains—making concentric circles around the massive rocks. She was not at all interested. My carsick and easily terrified mother would often lie down in the back seat as I sat up front with my father help-ing him by reading maps.

Sometimes we would stop at lookouts and my father would point out features of the landscape. "See those rocks over there?" he began as we perched high above the Grand Canyon. "The bottom is the oldest part of the whole earth and as it gets closer to where we are now, it keeps changing. Layer by layer." I was fascinated by the colors and striations of the rocks. He continued, "Scientists—geologists who study rocks—can tell us a lot about the conditions on earth during different time periods. Even millions of years ago."

I was stunned. "So, Papa, all of this changing has brought us to right here right now?" I said, leaning down and patting the ground I was standing on. He nodded.

"You see, Sylvia," he said while staring out at the impos-sibly huge chasm before us, "life is sort of like this. We keep changing and adding layers upon layers of living. Different conditions produce different effects on us—right from our beginnings." We stared silently for a few minutes, then he took my hand and we walked slowly back to the car where my mother was sound asleep in the back seat.

We traveled on across rivers and plains and deserts. I wrote down as much as I could about the changing landscape and the people I met—the kind waitresses, the Texaco men who often gave me lollipops, the motel clerks who delighted me with my very own tiny bars of Camay soap.

During the day this was a glorious adventure. At night, however, I was plagued by horrific dreams. I feared that I would become separated from my parents, and, unable to speak or understand English, I would never be able to reunite with them. When I awoke from these dreams, often crying and sweating, I would wake my mother and my father and cling to them for hours. They tried their best to reassure me that we would not be separated, but I didn't believe them. What if? What if?

And each night, the terrors returned. Deep in the heart of the vastness of Nebraska, I asked my father to teach me how to read the stars like the ancient sailors I had read about in books. I wanted to learn how to always find my way back to my parents. Although he was not knowledgeable in celestial navigation, he calmed me with stories of the constellations.

"We will always be with you, even when you get older and have your very own house and family and life. Remember the Grand Canyon? See, the layers built one on the other. They didn't go away—they added to the whole structure. You will always be able to find us because we are always part of you." He put his arm around my shoulders and I leaned into his side.

"See over there? That's Venus; it's a planet. And you can barely see it but another planet, Jupiter, is there too," he said, pointing to bits of light far away near the moon. And continued, "The ancient sailors and modern astronomers made maps of the skies—just like maps of the roads we're following. That way they could always tell where they were."

"It changes all the time, doesn't it, Papa?" I said wistfully and continued, "Nothing stays still in exactly the right spot, does it? Even when it feels perfect."

"No, it doesn't," he agreed and sighed.

I looked up at the vastness of the almost-black sky, dotted with pinpoints of thousands of lights. Stars. Planets. Always there but never in exactly the same place and exactly the same condition. Even mountains changed. Even the earth. Even me. Even my parents.

The world was beautiful. Wondrous. But I knew deep in my bones, even at the age of seven, the very fragile nature of our lives—how easily we can be torn from those we love by larger forces.

I know that still.

CHAPTER 10

ENCHANTMENTS

"I have always felt charged with the safekeeping
of all unexpected items of worldly and unworldly
enchantment, as though I might be held personally
responsible if even a small one were to be lost."

–E.B. White

"She died of a long illness," they told me when I asked
about my great-grandmother Anna. My mother remembered her from when as a child she lived in Poland. "Oh, she
was wonderful. I had typhus when I was seven, your age, and
she brought me back to health. My fever was so high she had
to put me in an ice bath to lower it. They thought I was going
to die."

I could not imagine such misery. It was 1957, I was seven

years old, and we were sitting around the big dining room table in Montevideo, Uruguay, with some of my family's old Polish friends. Although their Spanish—my language at the time—was halting and my grandmother would have to translate some words and phrases for me, even then as a young child I loved their stories and the word-pictures they would paint of that old world they had left.

In 1930 my grandmother had managed to escape the horrors of Poland with her two small children in tow, but not before having to say a painful farewell to her beloved mother-in-law. My mother remembered (in Polish) her grandmother's parting words, "Sara, you be a good girl and listen to your mother. She will help you to a better life. It is not safe for us here. Be very brave." She knew she'd never see her grandchildren again.

The 1940s brought horrors to the extended family in Poland, with many killed in concentration and labor camps and many others simply murdered in their homes. All communication had stopped. It was not until many years later, the early 1950s, that several of the remaining relatives and friends were able to emigrate. Some came to Uruguay, where the little country welcomed them with services to help them get jobs, learn the language, and find housing. And now, here they were, sitting around the big wooden table talking and laughing.

"Remember that time Solomon was so full of beer that he couldn't get up the stairs and Herman tried to help him but they both ended up rolling down? Achhh, what silliness that was," they chuckled. And then, "We didn't know how bad it was going to get later. No one really knew," as they grew suddenly solemn and quiet.

I took that lull as an opportunity to ask about my great-grandmother and was told of her death. And then they continued, "But it was an amazing thing when she died. Back then, in 1939, it was instructed that Jews were not allowed formal burials. They were just dumped into mass graves. But not your great-grandmother."

"Why not?" I asked.

They continued, "Because all of her life she helped the poor. If she had one piece of bread left she would give half of it to the poor and half to her family and she herself would eat nothing. If she had two pieces of cloth she would sew a dress for a desperate child."

"So, she helped the Jewish community," I mused.

"No," I was told, "not just that community. She helped everyone who needed her help. The poor people of the village of all religions loved her so much that when she died, they found a way to buy a coffin for her and then they carried it in a long procession to the old Jewish cemetery. It was the first burial there in years. There must have been more than a hundred people walking together. Even the soldiers on watch did not disturb the ceremony.

"No one had ever seen anything like that before. A Jewish woman carried with so much dignity! We knew, all of us, we knew that this was the last moment we could all honor goodness in the world."

One of them patted my small hand. "Sylvia, we tell you the truth of our history. We are here now to tell this, but we will not be forever. Someday, you tell the stories so the world never forgets." I nodded.

And then these old Polish people, survivors of unimaginable suffering and grief, cast their heads down with long, heavy sighs. Even as a child I felt their sighs in my bones.

Later, amidst the regained laughter about past silliness while from the record player came songs unfamiliar to my ears, while they danced—galloping around the kitchen then dissolving into chairs with giggles like young kids—while they drank beer and wine and reveled in newfound Coca-Cola ("Ayyy, Malka, look at these bottles! So elegant!"), I watched in astonishment.

"So many bad things happened, but still they can be happy. How?" I asked my grandmother when she came to sit for a moment next to me.

She smiled. "You hear that phrase they say when they raise their glasses? It's 'L'chaim' and it means 'to life.' It means, my dear girl, that as long as there is life, there is cause for celebration."

And then she grabbed my hand and pulled me into the big circle of dancing.

CHAPTER 11

FAIR

"I could have danced all night, I could have danced all night, and still have asked for more!" I sang at the top of my lungs while flouncing around the living room, dining room, hallway. It was 1958, I was eight years old, and I had just come back from seeing my very first Broadway show, *My Fair Lady* with Julie Andrews and Rex Harrison. My parents had taken me to the Saturday matinee where I wore my best blue and white dress with a round collar emblazoned with tiny flowers, white socks with lace edging, shiny black shoes, white gloves, and a sturdy navy blue spring coat.

My parents joined in my romp around the house as we danced and sang until, exhausted, we all collapsed in a heap on the worn, green sofa. Both my mother and I had experienced some trouble understanding parts of the dialogue of the show since we just learned the English language a year ago, so we had barraged my American father with questions all the way home. But we had no trouble with the songs and the costumes and the spectacular sets. It was all gorgeous.

Thirty years later, in 1988, I put the video into the VCR so my mother and I could watch Audrey Hepburn in the movie version of that show. My father had been unusually ill recently; my daughter, husband, and I had just moved from Maryland to New Jersey to be closer to my parents; and having just finished my PhD, I was embarking on a new phase of my career. There was a lot of anxiety, of both the good and the difficult varieties, in all of our lives. My mother was depressed.

"Remember how much fun it was when we first saw the show?" I asked her, trying to animate her a bit. And I continued, "I heard the movie is great fun. So, let's watch it this afternoon." My mom nodded in silent agreement.

The story seemed quite the same. The same songs, beautiful costumes, and lovely backgrounds. Eliza Dolittle still sold violets and mused about having a warm place to live and someone to take care of her. She still wanted to make a better life for herself by getting speech lessons in order to sound more posh and have a chance at a better job of some sort. Henry Higgins still made a bet with his friend that as an elocution specialist he would be able to pass her off as a high-class lady within a certain period of time.

In short, he would teach her to be someone she was not. To fit in.

I had not remembered his arrogance. Or her fears of disaster. Or his disregard for any of her dignity. Or his blatant dismissal of any of her requests or needs. He was a man on a mission to shape this "creature" who had come into his life and he did so by removing all traces of the real Eliza and replacing her with his ideal of an upper-class woman who might do his bidding. For quite a while she resisted these machinations.

Of course, the story has her ultimately falling in love with him. And we are to somehow assume that his becoming "accustomed to her face" meant that he fell in love with her. She tries to leave in the end, tired of his arrogance and pride, but returns, only to have him still unable to show any love but rather ask her offhandedly where his slippers were.

At the end of the film my mother and I were speechless for a few minutes. Then, with more energy than I'd seen in her for quite some time, she sat up tall and declared that while she still loved the songs and costumes, the actual plot was terrible. "Women need to know they have choices. They do not have to endure abusive relationships," she began. And she continued, "You know, for months before you were born I was convinced I would name you Nora. I was sure you were going to be a girl and I had just seen the Ibsen play, *A Doll's House*. Nora was the first woman I had seen in a play that took control of her own life."

This was a shock to me. My mother did not like to read and she often wondered aloud how on earth she had a daughter who was a literature professor. Poems and novels and plays were never discussed or even brought up in conversations.

"Mom," I said, "I never knew this. I mean Ibsen? You saw an Ibsen play in Uruguay?"

"Yes," she responded, "and it was magnificent. My friend Sarah and I cheered when at the end Nora just left her husband and kids and all the lies that society was making her live with. I felt trapped by so much, but Nora got free."

I nodded, remembering my mother's abusive father; her first husband, Harry, who would desert her and leave her penniless with an infant and whom the law at that time would not let her divorce—only men had that power.

She continued, "I didn't like that Nora left her children, but she had to endure so much and she found a way to make her own life. Her own life!"

"But you named me Sylvia," I chuckled, confused by this new information.

"Ah," she smiled, "after my contractions started and they wheeled me into the labor room I heard the most beautiful music on the radio. It was the ballet *Sylvia*. The announcer explained the story as it was going along. Sylvia was a strong character. When she comes into the scene there are drums and trumpets and all sorts of powerful instruments. Love caused her a few problems later on"—now she winked at me as we both laughed remembering my own past dealings with love—"but she remained boldly true to herself. So, to everyone's surprise, when you were born—with your triumphant loud cries of life—I named you Sylvia."

I leaned forward to take the tape out of the VCR, place it back in its container, and ready it for a return to Blockbuster. "Were you disappointed that we watched the film, Mom?" I asked, hoping that it hadn't brought back her sadness.

"No," she answered, vigorously shaking her head. "It's good to remember some things about life. It's good to remember that even though it's not easy, we have choices to be like Eliza, or Nora, or . . ." now she grabbed my hand in hers, "or like Sylvia."

CHAPTER 12

A STUDENT STORY: MARY

A few weeks ago we had a Zoom conference. "Dr. Baer, I just want to apologize for not turning in my last paper (due yesterday). It's been a bit . . ." At this point loud crying could be heard behind her. Then a crash: metallic sounding, like pots and pans. Then a half-diapered toddler ran into the room sobbing. Margaret seamlessly reached down, picked up the child, and placed them on her lap and continued. "My mother is ill with congestive heart failure. I'm helping to take care of her because we can't really afford any home care. My dad passed away two years ago of a drug overdose and had used up the family savings on his habit. My two other kids are sick with a stomach bug and my husband has been in the hospital for two weeks with COVID complications—he had cancer and even after three shots is suffering badly. I just want to say I'm really embarrassed that I haven't gotten that to you yet and understand if you don't accept it for being a few days late. It's my responsibility. I just wanted to explain"—her eyes filled with un-spilled tears—"I just don't want you to think I'm being lazy."

The child was now asleep in her arms. Margaret reached up and pushed a wisp of hair away from her face. Now her large blue eyes were earnest and soft. In the two previous courses she had taken with me she showed herself to be a brilliant thinker and writer. I knew very little of her home life, but I knew she wanted passionately to be a high school English teacher. "Oh, I love books so much. I want everyone to experience the mind-traveling that they have to offer," she had told me.

Now I looked at her directly and responded: "What you are doing is the opposite of lazy. You are demonstrating perseverance in the face of overwhelming odds. You are not giving up. You are facing your challenges head-on and working against impossible barriers. And you are succeeding. How wonderful it would be for you to have the luxury of being a full-time student—the time to read and think and dream and analyze and experiment. But you have more than full-time demands and responsibilities and still you are working to make a better life for yourself and your family and your world. I am impressed and humbled by your dedication and power. Write your paper when you can. I look forward to reading it."

The following week Margaret turned her paper in—with a heartfelt thank you note. The essay? It examined the tension between the romantic and the realist in Don Quixote, and how to live a rich and full life one must travel the road of both and learn how to follow dreams while balancing the harshness that life sometimes puts in our way.

She earned a well-deserved A and my gratefulness for the opportunity to be a small part of her journey.

CHAPTER 13

KIND

"My mom says she has to be nice to you 'cause you're poor and it's not your fault. So, she has to be nice. It's called 'charity.' But she says you still can't swim in the pool because you're dirty and live with Brazilians."

My friend Jane was explaining things to me. It was March 1959, I was nine years old, and we were in San Paulo, Brazil. We had moved there in February; this was the fourth country I had lived in, and Portuguese was going to be my third language after my first language, Spanish (Uruguay and Argentina), and then English (United States). My dad was an entrepreneur and here in San Paulo he was starting two companies: a competitor to Fritos and also a textile factory. He wanted to live near his work, so against the advice of some friends, we did not settle in the American enclave of the city. He would also tell me, "If we're going to live in a country, we need to know about it. Not just from books—that's like being outside and looking through a window—but by being a part of it—the food, the sounds, the language, the people. Life."

Concerned that I might get behind in my studies, my parents did, however, enroll me in the exclusive private American "Graded School." I made friends easily and had lots of partners for games and activities during recess. After school, though, became a problem. No one was able to come to my house to play. And Jane was the only friend who invited me to her house. Since the school was perfectly positioned near the American enclave, this afternoon Jane and I walked to her house after classes.

I met her mother, who looked to me like a movie star. She was blond and tall with perfectly manicured hands and wore bracelets on her arms that jangled happily as she handed me a tall glass of lemonade. "Why, it's strange," she said offhandedly as she walked away, "you look perfectly normal."

This confused me, so I asked Jane what she meant. Jane continued, "No one else will have you over because the other moms aren't as kind as mine." I thought about this as I sipped my drink and munched my cookie, but soon forgot all about it while we ran around playing tag and skipping rope in the bright sunshine.

At five o'clock my father came to pick me up. Jane and I were waiting in her front parlor. He stepped out of one side of a black limousine, and I saw someone else step out of the other side. And then I heard Jane's mom gasp: "Oh my. Is that . . . ?" I didn't hear the rest because I suddenly recognized Uncle Briggs. He wasn't my real uncle, but I was given to understand that he was the reason my dad had moved to Uruguay after finishing his graduate work in economics. Uncle Briggs, who, like my dad, was from Massachusetts, was the American ambassador to Uruguay when my dad had finished graduate school and was looking for a place to start his career in international business, and so he encouraged my dad to start there. He even helped him set up the Schick Razor company there and often invited him and my mom to events.

When I was five years old I met him for the first time and took an immediate liking to the smiling kind man who always had wonderful stories full of adventure. He loved plants and animals and buildings, and told me long involved tales of his travels to other parts of the world. And always when I visited, his staff had delicious ice cream for me—strawberry, my favorite kind.

He left Uruguay a few years ago and was now the American ambassador to Brazil.

"Uncle Briggs!" I yelled as I ran to hug him.

"Sylvia," my dad admonished, "remember your manners." So I stepped back and curtsied as I had been taught to do (and had to continue doing until the age of twelve), lowered my head a tad, and said, "Ambassador Briggs, it's a pleasure to see you again." I looked up and saw his eyes and we both dissolved into laughter.

"Mickey Mouse"—his nickname for me—"how delightful to see you! Your dad and I were doing some work and so here we are to gather you up and take you for ice cream. And who is this?" Jane had appeared behind me with her mom behind her.

"This is my friend."

Suddenly Jane's mom bubbled over: "Ambassador Briggs, I'm so pleased to meet you. I'm Margery Wilson, Joseph Wilson's wife."

I was even more confused. She seemed befuddled. And she introduced herself to my father and told him what a delight it was to have me visiting her home. My dad smiled and invited Jane to come for ice cream with us.

"No, she can't," I explained loudly and matter-of-factly because my father apparently didn't understand the rules. "Her mom says she's not allowed, none of my school friends are, because we're dirty and live with Brazilians."

"Is that so?" Uncle Briggs said, as I saw Mrs. Wilson's skin turn a bright red.

"Well, now, that is a shame," my father continued. "I was hoping Jane would be able to join us." I said a quick goodbye as he ushered me into the car.

Later, while we ate our ice cream, I asked my dad and Uncle Briggs why my friends' parents thought we were dirty and why they thought living with Brazilians was bad.

"Sylvia," my dad sighed, "there are people in this world that are convinced that they are better than others just because of where they were born or how much money they have or who their parents are. But that's not important in our family. What is important is honoring and respecting every-one. We have to learn how to understand and value each and every person as individuals." Uncle Briggs nodded.

The following week brought a barrage of invitations to school friends' houses. I discovered, though, that as much as I liked playing with my friends at school, the Brazilian friends I was making in my neighborhood were a lot of fun also. Their houses were full of music and color and delicious food and with their help I started speaking Portuguese proficiently. In fact, a few months later, when at a fancy dinner I met the new ambassador, Mr. John Cabot, I was able to curtsy, lower my head a tad, and say both "pleased to meet you" and "prazer em conhecê-lo" with only a hint of a giggle.

And Mr. John Cabot met my eyes, laughed, and said, "I believe you and I are going to be good friends."

U.S. Embassy
Montevideo
4th of July —
1952

CHAPTER 14

A STUDENT STORY: HERMAN

He was in my American Literature class several years ago. It was during our discussion of the waves of immigrants from Ireland and Italy in the nineteenth and early twentieth centuries and the horrific prejudice and hatred that they endured and the various works of art and literature that they inspired, that I learned his story.

He told me.

He was born in and lived in a Central American country. The gangs who killed his mother, raped his sister and then killed her, and hung his father (a local journalist) publicly, saw him bleeding on the street and assumed he was dead. He was seven. American missionaries eventually found him foraging for food behind trash dumps. They took care of him until they were forced out of the country two years later. Miraculously he managed to survive long enough to be useful on cargo docks where he learned about ships.

He stowed away when he was fourteen and landed in America. He had little idea of how anything worked here, but he knew some English thanks to those missionaries. All too quickly he learned that in order to stay he would need "to be legal." That meant official documents, and that meant lawyers. Since he didn't even have money for food, hiring a lawyer was out of the question.

First, he would have to earn the money. He worked in factories, backs of restaurants, fish processing plants, just to survive. At night he would study in a place that he called "heaven on earth"—the library. One librarian connected him to organizations that taught him basic skills, another connected him to soup kitchens and shelters, another gave him books of poetry. All saved his life, he said. Eventually he was able to do the paperwork, hire a lawyer, and become a legal resident.

He met the love of his life who convinced him to keep going to school. She cleaned houses and worked day shifts at convenience stores while he worked night shifts and weekends. And so, he landed in my class a while back, on his road to becoming a social worker. A brilliant, soft-spoken, kind-hearted bear of a man, I was sure of his future success and proud of his choice to help others.

His wife contacted me recently. Herman had always loved a small volume of Whitman's poetry I had given him before he graduated. He had it with him in his jacket when he died, she said. The lawyer who had taken their money to make them legal residents was a crook and created a ruse to get them bogus resident papers and then he disappeared.

They were penniless and now they found their documents were unsound. They needed to get more money for a new legal road. But in the process Herman was picked up by immigration authorities while he worked at night. They left his wife and their three-year-old daughter behind. He died in the process of deportation—she didn't tell me how or why.

But in the wake of this tragedy, she has finally found a way to get documents that are clearly legal. She's now safe. Their daughter, she tells me, still cries every day for her "papa," who would gently and playfully carry her on his shoulders, his back, and who wanted so much to make our world better.

CHAPTER 15

JULIA MAE JACKSON

"Julia Mae Jackson, you sit right there and don't leave this room until I am done. Do you hear me?"

It was August 1960, I was ten years old, and I heard Mrs. Jackson's stern warnings as I got off of the elevator onto the lobby floor of our New York City apartment building. Mrs. Jackson's rich, dark caramel skin usually folded itself in what seemed to me like commas around her full face. But today her lips were pursed, there were soft beads of sweat on her brow, and her skin seemed tight across her cheeks. She was wagging her finger in warning as she headed toward the stairs when she saw me.

"Good afternoon, Sylvia. That's my granddaughter sittin' over there. No one around to watch her today—had to bring her with me. I think she's 'bout your age. Gotta run. Need to clean the Darnoffs' place today." And off she went into the stairwell with the heavy door slamming loudly behind her.

I saw Julia Mae Jackson open a red bag that looked a lot like my blue one that I used for school. And then she took out a book. I got closer and saw it was one I had just finished reading, *Little Women*. She looked up and saw me staring.

"Hi," I offered, "I just read that book too. D'you like it?"

She shrugged and said, "Well, I think that I like Jo, but I'm angry about the end."

I squealed, "Me too! Why does she marry the professor when she spent the whole time saying how she doesn't want to get married? Does she just do it 'cause everyone thinks she's supposed to?"

Now Julia Mae Jackson chimed in, "And then she has kids and you know she'll never be able to have time to write again."

"Or read," I continued. Julia Mae Jackson and I both shook our heads and sighed in deep regret at bad decisions made by a beloved character.

And then noticing my bunched up right hand, "Hey, whatcha got there?" she asked.

I showed her my new Pinky ball. "Got it for twenty cents yesterday. I wanted to buy a Spaldeen but they cost more and . . ." I trailed off.

Julia Mae Jackson reached into her red bag and her brown hand pulled out a Pinky ball just like mine and said, "My grandma got me this brand new one yesterday. I didn't want to tell her I was trying to save up for the Spaldeen. I knew we didn't have the money." We both nodded. She continued, "It's sort of like the whole March family. I mean their dad was off to war and the whole of 'em didn't have much."

We both nodded again and I jumped in, "My dad's off to start a business in Venezuela. He's worried a lot. My mom too. I'm trying to not want anything at all. I saved a long time for my new Pinky ball."

We both sat in silence for a minute and then she started bouncing her ball on the linoleum floor. I joined in, rhythm chanting a familiar game: "A my name is Alice and my husband's name is Al and we come from Alabama and we sell apples," as I swung my leg over the ball, careful not to lose the bounce. Her turn, "B my name is Barbara and . . ." We made it all the way through the alphabet taking turns and collapsed on the big lobby chairs in giggles.

"My dad isn't home either," Julia Mae Jackson said as we quieted down. "We don't know where he is. Left home one day when I was too little to remember and just never came back. My momma works in a hair place up in Harlem and my grandma cleans houses. They tell me I've got to go to school and get a good education so I can be somebody of my own and not need other people's money."

I nodded in understanding. "My mom and grandmother tell me the exact same thing. My first dad wasn't any good. He left when I was tiny. I got a new dad who is wonderful, but he's always worried about money."

She nodded and continued, "Know how to play stoop ball?" Of course I did! We jumped up and went outside and laid out the rules, the points (100 to catch a pointer—when it hits the edge of the step—on the fly!), and the timing. It was a close game.

We were playing to 300 and just when I was about to catch a 100-pointer, Mrs. Jansen came dashing out the front door and interrupted me with a question. "Who is this you're playing with, Sylvia?" she asked with an angry face, and then continued, "I've never seen her 'round here before."

I smiled. "This is Julia Mae Jackson, Mrs. Jackson's granddaughter. She's my new friend." Mrs. Jansen swirled her skirt around her and huffed off into the building.

We tried to resume our game but pretty soon, my mother came outside following Mrs. Jansen and said, "What's wrong, Sylvia? I understand there's a problem."

I was stumped. "Nothing's wrong. We were just playing stoop ball and . . ."

Now Mrs. Jansen jumped in. "We don't like that sort of . . . of person, playing here in front of everyone," she stammered while looking directly at my friend. And then continued, "There are standards to be kept, you know. Dignity must be maintained."

My mother looked at my confused face and then at my friend's bent-down head and sighed. "I will take care of this," she said firmly enough for Mrs. Jansen to swoop back inside clutching her handbag tightly.

Then my mother sat on the middle of a step and patted the spaces on either side of her, motioning us to sit down.

"Mom, I don't think we did anything wrong. I don't understand . . ." I sputtered.

Julia Mae Jackson nodded and said, "I don't either but this happens a lot. My grandma says that folks don't like my dark skin because they don't know the person inside of it. And if they did, they'd be all over themselves liking me."

My mother smiled. "Your grandma is absolutely right. Now you girls stay right here while I go inside and get some cookies, OK?" We nodded happily.

A few minutes later my mother came out with Mrs. Jackson right next to her. "Mrs. Jackson has graciously agreed to stay for dinner tonight with her granddaughter. I think we can all use an easy supper and some fun." We clapped in delight.

After a simple meal of my mom's best spaghetti and meatballs ("Look, Mom, see? Julia Mae Jackson eats it just like I do!), lots of laughter, and a game of Parcheesi, they left. "We need to leave while it's still light out," Mrs. Jackson explained. My mother nodded in understanding.

Later, as I hugged my mom and declared it to be a spectacular night, I said, "I think maybe Julia Mae Jackson and I are twins. We are so alike in every possible way!"

"Yes, you are," she affirmed, "yes, you are." And then with a sigh, "Let's hope the world soon learns to see that."

CHAPTER 16

NOURISHMENT

"I did something terribly wrong, I just know it," I sputtered in between sobs.

It was a Saturday in early January 1960, I was nine years old, living in Passaic, New Jersey, and sitting in Patty's (my best friend's) living room. She had convinced me to tell her mother my problem.

"Did you commit a sin?" Mrs. Ingrassia asked, handing me a glass of water and a fresh white embroidered hanky. I wasn't sure what a sin actually was, but I knew what I had done was against the law. I had just become a brand new citizen and read all about the laws in the handbook I needed to study ahead of time.

"I think I might be a criminal and I don't know what to do," I choked out.

Suddenly, their front door opened and in walked Patty's

sister, who was a brand-new nun. Two months ago Patty had told me about her. "Well, her name used to be Therese but when she took her vows she became 'Sister Philomena.' She said it was the name of the patron saint of children so that's what her life is about. I still think she's just my stupid sister but I'm not allowed to say that anymore," she had said, rolling her eyes while we both dissolved into a fit of giggles.

"Sister Philomena," Mrs. Ingrassia said, "Patty's friend Sylvia is very upset because she thinks she's done something terrible. I don't know what it is yet but maybe you can help us."

Sister Philomena sat down in a chair facing me directly. I had no experience with nuns, but my parents had taken me to see the Broadway show *The Sound of Music* the previous month so I knew that they helped people figure things out. I hung my head and stared at the floor before beginning.

I told them about saving up one dollar and thirty-two cents and yesterday after school going to our local corner grocery store, Kurwitzki's, to buy some special candy and soda treats. I continued, "I was walking down the back section and I saw a woman with a baby. I had seen her before, in the park last month, on my way home from school. I remembered because it was really, really cold and she took off her coat and wrapped it around a baby she was holding. She looked like she was shaking and her clothes were all . . . well, they looked really torn. She saw me looking and she almost ran away."

I stopped for a sip of water and to blow my nose and saw Mrs. Ingrassia and Sister Philomena look at each other. I continued, "So I recognized the lady when I saw her in the store. I could hear her trying to quiet the baby by singing but it wasn't in English or Spanish or Portuguese, and those are the only languages I know. She was really thin and the baby was wrapped up in shabby torn pieces of cloth. But then I saw it."

I stopped to take a deep breath and continued, "She put two cans of baby formula in her pockets. I saw her do it. And she walked out quickly."

"And what did you do then?" Sister Philomena asked me.

"Well, I wasn't sure what to do but it seemed to me that the baby needed food and she couldn't afford it and she needed help and no one should go hungry and . . . Well, I didn't report it. I know I was supposed to but I just couldn't. The law tells me to do it, but something inside told me not to."

I took another deep breath and kept going. "I didn't know how much the formula cost and Mr. Kurzwitski shouldn't lose that money either, so I just left my one dollar and thirty-two cents on the counter and walked out. By then she had disappeared. I was going to tell my mom but when I got home she was really worried about my dad who was in Venezuela on business and there was some sort of revolution there right now. I couldn't upset her more with this problem. I could hardly sleep all night and food just won't go down my throat today."

Now Mrs. Ingrassia had a phone book in her hand and Sister Philomena moved closer to me and began asking me for more descriptions of the woman, assuring me that nothing bad would happen. I described her as best I could. But then to try to calm me Patty began singing a snippet of a lullaby her grandmother had sung to her and I jumped up. "That's it, that's the song she was singing to her baby," I exclaimed.

Mrs. Ingrassia picked up the phone and started dialing, Sister Philomena ran out the door yelling that she'd be back in a minute, and Patty and I were left to ourselves on the worn red velvet couch. "What do you think is going to happen, Patty?" I asked, sighing deeply. She shrugged. We both sat quietly and waited.

Within half an hour women started coming into the house, arms filled with things. Cans of baby formula, two winter coats, piles of cloth diapers, hats, gloves, baby clothes, all began filling the dining room table. It was like a miracle. Patty and I were given the job of sorting things into neat piles.

And then more than an hour later an even bigger miracle happened. Sister Philomena came in with the woman and baby, whom she was able to find by asking folks from the church and neighborhood. In a language I didn't understand she introduced her to everyone. Patty translated for me. Her name was Angelica. She and her husband, Antonio, had immigrated from Sardinia in Italy in late August. He had been promised a good job in a factory in exchange for their small savings. And even though Angelica was very pregnant at the time, they came eager for a new start in life only to find that no such factory existed. Antonio found small work but the baby Maria's birth took all of his earnings. They found one room to live in over a small gas station but food was scarce and they had not yet learned enough English to be understood.

Within the next hour a big pot of pasta was boiling on the stove, Mrs. Ingrassia's neighbor Mrs. Maratelli came over with tomato sauce–laced meatballs, and Joe Mondano—a foreman at the local Continental Can Company—had been summoned to fetch Antonio and it was clear he would be offered a line job at the plant.

Songs were sung, food was eaten (my first taste of a cannoli) and stories were told. Angelica came over to me. "Grazie," she said and then very hesitantly, "thank you." She hugged me, and we both smiled.

Days later my father came safely home. My mother's nerves had nearly snapped by then. I learned there had been an uprising in the region where he was staying, but local villagers had given him a safe hiding spot. "It was very brave of them," my father explained, "because the rebels were after foreigners, thinking that they were invading the country and taking their resources. I was going to be killed. But kind people saw that I was doing no harm but I was in danger, so they felt they had to help. And I'm so glad they did!"

"It seems to me, Daddy," I began, "that when people really take the time to listen to each other and to help each other, it makes everything better." And I told him about Angelica and Antonio and baby Maria and Sister Philomena and Mrs. Ingrassia and the entire community.

His bright blue eyes looked directly at me as he said, "Don't forget any part of this, Sylvia. Always remember that most of the world is filled with good people who want to help others. Don't be dismayed (a new word for me) by those who want to harm. There are so few of them that if all the rest can just work together, wonderful things can happen. Sometimes it only takes one person to get things going."

CHAPTER 17

GIVING THANKS

"Look, I already told you thank you. What else do you want from me? You're always like this—you do some little favor and then you just want me to bow and scrape and act all deliriously grateful every time I see you," Mrs. Collins from 3L yelled as she angrily folded a fresh-from-the-dryer bedsheet.

It was late June of 1963; I was thirteen years old and in the laundry room of our apartment building. It seemed unusually busy that day, but I was avoiding other tasks and was happy to linger awhile, to wait for an available washing machine.

Just last week we had my eighth-grade graduation and already I was planning for a busy summer. But first I had to write thank you notes to all of the friends and distant relatives who sent me presents. It was a tedious task but one I knew was important. Having to sound enthusiastic about formal white, elbow-length gloves, or a large pink and purple elephant brooch was hard work. In truth, I resented some of the time-consuming tasks. But then I felt guilty for feeling that way. Folks were kind enough to send me gifts and I should happily thank them. But still, the battle raged within me.

So the argument between Mrs. Collins and her sister, Mrs. Briggs (4K), was especially interesting to me that day. Now Mrs. Briggs countered her sister, "You gotta be grateful when I do something for you. It took a lot of time and I could've been doing my hair or nails. But instead I took care of your dog. I mean, I deserve some recognition for giving up my time. And let's face it, you never do nothing for me, do you? It's always me doing for you."

All their laundry folded, the two sisters left the area, still irritated, sounding like angry geese honking and sniping at each other. Mrs. Kerwitz (2A) and Miss Hotlzman (3C), who had been sitting on either side of me reading magazines while waiting for machines to empty, got up and started transferring their wet laundry to the now-available dryers. I put my gym clothes and underwear and shorts into the washer, poured in Tide soap powder, put my quarter in the slot, and sat back down.

"Sylvia, you look confused," Mrs. Kerwitz exclaimed.

I nodded as I looked up into her soft wrinkled face; wisps of gray hair—having escaped the tight bun on the back of her head—strayed onto her cheeks and forehead. "I am," I said. "I don't think I understand the idea of thanking others very well. Of course we should do it, but how much is enough? I just don't know."

Even though she was finished loading the machine and on her way out of the room, Miss Holtzman, a woman about my mother's age who worked as a nurse in our nearby hospital, jumped into the conversation. "I think that when people do something for you they shouldn't expect anything back. You do good things because you want to—because you think it's the right thing to do, not because you want anything in return." And then starting to round the corner to the hallway she finished, "Good deeds are their own reward."

Mrs. Kerwitz shook her head, looked at me, and said, "Well, I certainly agree with that idea. You shouldn't expect anything back from having helped anyone or having done some small or large favor. But, you see, we're all human and I think we need to feel our lives matter. It's hard to do that totally on our own. It's sometimes important to know that what we do matters to someone else."

I nodded. I could understand this. And then she concluded, now having inserted a dime into the dryer and gathering herself to go back upstairs: "You know when you give of yourself it helps someone else and the good feeling helps you also. The same is true when you acknowledge a favor, because you remind yourself that someone cared enough to do something for you. And in thanking them, you show you care as well. You see, Sylvia, I think the whole world revolves in its very center, on the love and appreciation we show each other however we can."

She was right. I knew it. Down to my very bones I could feel her words. My card-writing task ahead seemed lighter and full of promise.

I could hear her slow footsteps shuffling down the corridor amid the whirring and clanging of the machines around me—water and heat cleansing the dirt and grime of daily wear—helpfully rinsing and fluffing to make way for more usefulness.

June 24, 1963

To my darling Sylvia,
   This graduation marks
the end of "Chapter I."
   One's life is a history book
written on time instead of
paper and with character
instead of pen and ink.
   May all the following
Chapters be as full of happiness
and joy as this first one.
   Deepest love
      your Father

CHAPTER 18

LINES

I knew it was wrong, but I did it anyway. It was January 1960, I was almost ten years old, and we had recently returned from living in Brazil for two years. English was my second language (after Spanish) and then I had to learn to manage in Portuguese. Back in the U.S. and in fifth grade now, I had fallen into English easily, but some words and phrases still eluded me. Generally my American dad helped clarify things, but right now he was away on business and I was relying on my best friend, Patty, for help.

"I don't get it. Why is it called a 'party line' when it's just a phone and it's not a party at all?" I asked her as we munched on our sandwiches at lunch.

I was referring to the phone system at Mrs. Cohen's house where we were living temporarily. Mrs. Cohen's sons had married and moved away and she was left in her house alone.

As a favor to her friend, a distant relative of ours, two years ago she had agreed to let us stay with her for a few months. After that, we left for Brazil and two new business ventures for my dad, but now we were back again. The phone system that she had installed to save money while we were away meant that several families shared one phone line. In general we had no idea who the other people were. It was supposed to be anonymous. You would pick up the receiver and if someone else was talking, you were honor bound to hang up. This was the code that everyone accepted and was expected to live by.

"It's 'cause there are lots of different parties on the line. Parties can mean people," Patty explained.

And then I confessed to her, "Sometimes I listen to other conversations. It's fun to hear what they talk about. Usually it's sort of boring—about dinner and shopping—but once in a while there's a real story."

"You shouldn't do that," Patty admonished me, "that's eavesdropping and my mom says that's wrong to do."

She was right. Just last month I had studied really hard and passed my citizenship test and vowed, before the judge, to uphold the laws of the land. And here I was doing a wrong thing.

But I was so interested.

Mrs. Cohen did not know about my listening, but in general she did not approve of me. I could hear her talking to my mother in the back kitchen as I hunched on the stairs: "You need to discipline her, Sara. She will never understand right from wrong if you don't," and "You don't give her rules. She needs to have absolute rules," and "Look at how she comes home from school—she's always a mess. Her socks are slouched, and her skirt is messy with mud, and her hair falls out all over the place. That's not right for a girl. Girls need to look tidy and clean all the time."

Well, she wasn't wrong. I never remember having rules or limits. My parents simply expected me to do the right thing. And it was true, my mother would continually sigh and complain about my appearance. When my father was home he would temper her anger. "Let her be herself, Sara, she enjoys life. Let her explore. Boys can do it, why not girls?" he would tell her.

But on this day in January, with my father far away in Venezuela, when I picked up the phone, what I heard was different. The voice on the other end sounded urgent. "Please, Momma, let me come and stay with you. I'm afraid here. I'm scared." And the reply was, "I'm not getting in the middle. You made your choice. You can't just leave your husband. No one else will marry you. It'll be a disgrace." And then a click and the voice started sobbing before her phone clicked off as well.

I did not know what to do with this information. If I said anything to my mother or Mrs. Cohen they would be angry at my bad behavior. But the voice needed help. I picked up the phone to call Patty for advice but heard the same voice again: "But Officer, he hits me. Yesterday he threw a bottle at me. I'm afraid. Help me please." And the reply, "Sorry, ma'am, but we can't get involved in domestic disputes," and he hung up. She stayed on the line again sobbing. I almost said something, but then "click," she had hung up.

I marched into the kitchen where Mrs. Cohen was chopping vegetables and my mother was putting a chicken in the oven. I hung my head and began, "I know I'm a disgrace, but I listened to the party line." Both women scowled at me. I looked up now. "I know I'm in trouble, but I don't care because someone needs help, and I don't know how to help her." Then I told them what I'd heard. All the details I could remember. Their faces changed and they both quickly began to act. "Mary Fran is over at the main switchboard. I'll find out who this is. I'll call from next door—from Gladys's house, she's got a private line." And so it went for the next hour with both women turned tornados of action. And then Gladys came to the house with bags and Mrs. O'Neil brought plates of food and then Mrs. Harper came with her husband, a construction worker. All assembled in our living room.

"Sylvia," Mrs. Cohen said, "you need to call this number. It's the woman you heard. No one will recognize your voice. But you can't say anything that someone else might hear suspiciously. So you say to her, 'Hi, this is Mary. We'll pick you up in fifteen minutes for that ladies' card party we planned this afternoon when we talked. Wait outside your front door. We will drive you.'" And so I did.

Within the hour Louise E. was in our living room looking tired and scared. Women scurried about bringing food to her and covering her with blankets. To my surprise, I was not sent away. I felt privileged to be part of this coming together—a helper line I called it. I heard her sad and terrifying story from my favorite bench in the corner. Then I heard them all help her formulate a plan which included staying with the

Harpers until other arrangements could be made. All shook their heads at the misguided nature of her mother, but then Mrs. Cohen spoke up.

"You know, sometimes we have things so ingrained in our thinking from years of being told what to do and how to think, that we don't even realize how wrong it is. How hurtful it is to others. And sometimes we have to accept that doing the appropriate thing isn't doing—without thinking—what we were told, but having the strength and good sense to do what is just and honorable and right."

And as she said this, Mrs. Cohen looked right at me.

After everyone left and my mother was helping me get ready for bed, Mrs. Cohen came into my room and for the first time ever, she hugged me. Then she looked me straight in the eye and said, "Sylvia Kuhner, you are an excellent and courageous citizen of this country and . . . ," now I was staring at her in astonishment, "I admire you."

CHAPTER 19

A STUDENT STORY: DANIEL AND MARTIN

"Why is he hiding under the desk?" I asked anxiously.

One of my most dedicated students, Daniel, had come to speak with me during my office hours late on a Wednesday afternoon in December. It was already dark outside at 4:30 and I was finishing paperwork when he walked in wearing his familiar white shirt ("Iron them every day—Mamma always taught me to iron and starch my shirts and my smile before I walk out the door.") with the gently fraying cuffs which he absentmindedly tugged under. During the semester I had learned that when he was ten his father died, and now Daniel, his young brother, and his two sisters lived with their mom in a one-bedroom apartment in a run-down housing project in Camden, NJ, a city which is miles away from the college. His mom worked the night shift at a local factory and had house-cleaning jobs during the day. Daniel himself worked a number of jobs but somehow (even though he had to take two buses and walk about a mile and a half as well) always was on time for our 9:20 AM American Literature class—eager with questions and ideas.

This particular afternoon he wanted to ask me a few things about his final paper, which he wanted to get "just right." As he walked in I noticed a young boy behind him, and then Daniel coached him: "It's OK, Martin, this is a fine lady. She's my professor and I'd like you to meet her. Remember what I taught you."

Shyly the young boy, about eight, stepped out from behind. He was dressed in a stiffly starched white shirt and crisp khaki pants. Gently he held out his hand. "Pleased to meet you, ma'am."

I shook his hand and said," Well, you must be Daniel's brother. He's told me how proud he is of how well you're doing in school. One day I'm sure you'll be in college also and doing just as well as your wonderful older brother." I smiled at them both, hopeful for their futures.

"Mom is at work so I thought maybe I would bring Martin in to my college and show him where he could study one day. He loves books so I took him to the library first."

Now Martin chimed in eagerly, "There are millions of books in that building. Millions! And they let you touch them and read them and even take them home." I looked questioningly at Daniel, who told me that in his neighborhood it was too dangerous to walk to the library and the classroom library was the only place Martin could get books.

"Except for Fridays," Martin interrupted.

"Fridays?"

"Yes. That's when Daniel brings me a brand new book. Every Friday. So now I make my own library in my corner. I got boxes and a top and I made a desk. And I found an old crate on the street and made that my library. And if you want you could come over and you can read my books," he blurted out eagerly.

I smiled and nodded. Daniel looked at me and spoke. "I want him to learn that the world is waiting for us. I want him to know that he's smart and capable and that he can lift himself up. And I want him to know that he's worth as many books as I can manage to buy him. I get paid on Thursdays, so Friday I stop at the bookstore and get him a book. I have extra time then so I just walk home and use my bus money for books."

Seven miles. He walks seven miles. Now he playfully addressed Martin, "So are you going to write me a good book report for my birthday next week? Maybe with pictures too?"

I smiled: "How old will you be, Daniel?"

"Nineteen."

At this Martin let out a howl of horrific pain. "Nooo. No. NO!!!!" he screamed and dove under my desk.

Daniel tried to coax him out. "I'll be fine. Don't worry." I was confused as Martin hid under the desk crying in pain. Daniel explained: "In our community, black men die young. Everyone says nineteen is the death year. Black men die around us every day. Our own daddy went out for groceries and was killed—it was two days before Martin was born. So now he's afraid I'm going to die."

I climbed under the desk and sat with the crying young boy and put my arm around him. "I can't promise you anything, Martin. But you know your brother is really smart. He's working very hard to get himself and your family a better life. I think he's really powerful, don't you? I'll bet he'll be just fine."

But even as I said those words, I wasn't sure I believed them. So much violence in the world every single day. So much fear. So much sacrifice and pain. And so much love.

Daniel reached down to help me up off the floor—I noticed his hastily patched shoes as he lifted me up. Then he reached for his brother and held him in his arms. "You and me, we're going to be just fine. Mamma named me for that man in the Bible who fought the lion and she named you for a great Black leader. We'll be fine. You'll see."

As they left, Martin turned to look at me and ran to give me a hug. I held him close and then gave him my large *Anthology of American Literature* book. "Wow, I can hardly carry this giant book," he told me with a big smile. When Daniel offered to hold it, Martin refused. "It's for me. It's all of America and I get to read it."

And so, dear friends, this student snapshot of twenty years ago (Can it be?) has this update: Daniel works as a school counselor in a large city where he has helped hundreds of kids from low-income households go to college. He finished his PhD last year and is writing his first book. And Martin? He's working for a congressman in Washington where his law degree has come in very handy. And every single Friday he brings home books for his two very young daughters.

CHAPTER 20

STAINS

"Careful, Sylvia, or you'll rub a giant hole into that," Mrs. Gianno chuckled. It was 1961 and eleven-year-old me was in the basement laundry room of our New York City apartment building. "Oh, Mrs. G., I'm so upset. Mrs. Ingrasso yelled at me again and I was trying so hard not to yell back that I spilled my orange soda all over my new white blouse. My mom isn't home, and I know if I don't get it right away it'll stain. I tried just water but that's not working. Not even with Tide."

"Well, you're right, we need to get this out as fast as possible, but I think more oomph is needed. Here, let me show you how to use bleach. This is cotton and bleach does work on cotton, just the white part, but not on other colors or fabrics. On colors and nylon and synthetics you would use lemon and baking soda and a little water and a hard brush. You must be mindful and understand what you will need for the problem at hand," she instructed. I listened carefully, did what she said, and slowly I could see the stains disappear. I rinsed thoroughly and the white part of my cotton blouse was all clean once again.

"Now," she continued while taking her own laundry out of the dryer and methodically folding it, "why was Mrs. Ingrasso yelling at you this time?"

I sighed and sat on a nearby stool and began, "She said I was a disgrace to the building because girls shouldn't be wearing shorts and my hair was a mess and my socks were all clumped up around my ankles and girls should always be presentable and I was never going to get a husband and my mother doesn't know how to handle me and . . ." Now I had gotten myself all upset again. "Mrs. G., I don't understand why she's always so angry. I try, I really try to smile and be polite. But even if I'm doing nothing she finds something mean to say to me." I sighed again, the deep sad sigh of a very confused child.

Mrs. G. leaned against the table where she now had three piles of freshly cleaned and sorted clothes and began, "Did you know about her terrible tragedy?" I did not. So she told me that Mrs. Ingrasso had left Italy in 1941 heading for America on a big ship with her husband and young daughter. It was a dangerous and long trip during the war but they felt sure they'd be safe when they got to their new country. Their young daughter, Teresa, developed a fever on board. Nothing helped her. She got sicker and sicker and eventually died. Because of the war, they had to bury Teresa at sea. When they disembarked onto Ellis Island there were only the two of them and their dreams of safety and happiness seemed crushed forever.

I nodded, remembering the deaths and hardships and fears of my own family—the stories they told me about the war and also my own journey to this new country. "But lots of people have tragedies. Why is she angry with me?" I asked. "I didn't hurt her."

Mrs. G. shook her gray head, soft curls tumbling across her forehead, and answered, "Ah, sometimes I don't think people actually understand why they're so angry. Maybe she sees you and remembers the girl she lost. Maybe she's so knotted up inside that nothing can unravel the pain. People don't understand even themselves when it becomes too much sadness to carry." She sighed and looked out the small ceiling-high windows at the single shaft of light streaming in.

"Here's something I think might make sense," she continued. "Anger can become like that soda on your blouse. If you don't work at it and use the right tools, it will become a permanent stain. You need to understand what it is first and then you know what to use to remove it. It takes understanding and hard work. And also, it takes wanting to get rid of the stain in the first place." I nodded. This made immediate sense to me.

"So how do I not be angry back?" I asked.

"Well," Mrs. G. replied, "when people yell at you or say mean things, you don't have to accept what they say. You can answer back. You can state your case and do so in a clear way. But once you start letting the anger rule you, once you lash out without thinking, once you start wishing bad things to happen to the other person, then you're in danger of making a stain in your heart. And you, Sylvia Kuhner, have a beautiful, clean heart," she said, giving me a warm hug and then carefully placing her laundry into the big wicker basket as I skipped out of the room holding my wet but pristine blouse.

Later that day when I told my mother, who had been struggling with her own difficulties and whose heart throughout her life held on to stains for far too long, about my interaction in the laundry room, she told me, "I don't think you know that Mrs. Gianno had two sons. Both boys were killed in the Korean War in 1950—the year you were born. Such a tragedy. Last year when a large group of Korean refugees came to the city no one could understand how she stepped forward to help. She raised money and found them good places to live. I'll never forget that when she came to ask for donations, she said: 'Everyone deserves to have a good life. Everyone deserves to be understood. If I carry hate in me then I diminish myself. No. I can't let that happen.'"

And my mother, whose face had held gray gloom for weeks, began to smile as she took my hand and continued, "It's hard for me sometimes. It really is. But I remember the last thing Mrs. G. told me that day. She said that love—love!—is the most powerful tool we have to rid the world of the stain of hate even if the only part we can change is within ourselves."

CHAPTER 21

VOICE

"Sylvia Judith Kuhner, get in the elevator now. Now!"

It was 1961, I was eleven years old, and we were living in an apartment in New York City. Mrs. Van Reisler, Mrs. Worthson, and Mrs. Langdon-Thorn were having a discussion in the lobby of our building. I overheard them. "She's a disgrace," and, "It's just too disgusting," and, "How can she just walk around like that?" and, "I think she's a horrible person." They were talking about Miss Margaret Harrison, who lived in 4G.

I had always gotten in trouble for talking too much and asking too many questions. "Sara, you're my good friend, but I'm afraid your daughter can't be in our ballet class any longer. She's too . . . she's too . . . disruptive," Señora Cantara had told my mother in 1956. I tried to explain that I only wanted to find out why we got to wear the tutus and boys didn't. And why stages were up high; and why Estrella always wore her hair in tight braids and how to make them and why Patricia had to wear glasses. Dancing seemed so unimportant compared to those questions.

Or when later that year my first-grade teacher had enough of my helping Pedro through his lessons and turning around to ask Perlita about her cat or leaning over to Juan to talk about yesterday's lunch. Eventually, at the end of her rope, Señora Gantos put tape over my mouth and sat me on the floor under my desk.

Later, Hortensia, my grandmother's helper in the hat store, listened as she sewed, and I told her yet another story about my predicament. "I try to behave, but I have so many questions in my head all the time. And I like talking to people. I like hearing what they say. I think people are the most important thing."

She sighed as she carefully stitched a soft blue bow to the side of a cream-colored cloche. "You have a very lively mind and a good voice. But you need to be sure that when you use it you are prepared for what happens next. And," now she stopped her work and looked directly at six-year-old me, "you should listen more than you talk. You can't learn about other people just by talking. You have to listen to what they say—to what they have experienced. That's how you really learn." I nodded. This made sense to me.

But now, five years later, standing in the lobby of our building, I could take it no longer and loudly interrupted the gossiping women. "Didn't Miss Harrison take care of your

Michael when he had measles? And didn't she stay with you when your husband was in the hospital and little Jimmy needed caring-for? And didn't she plan a whole birthday party for your twins because you were ailing from a sprained ankle?" I firmly told them, pointing at each one in turn. "Why are you being so horrible to her? What has she done to you except help you?" I really didn't understand.

"You see her, don't you?" Mrs. Worthson began, and flustered by my outburst she clutched her alligator bag close to her chest nervously snapping the clasp open then closed, open then closed—repeatedly. And continued, "She's . . . she's showing. I mean really! She's not married! We can't have those kind of morals in our building. She is sinning against God." All the women nodded in agreement.

My mother walked in from outside just as I loudly proclaimed, "What I know is that Miss Harrison is a kind person who helps everyone else. And if she's going to have a baby then it's another happy little life in the world. And . . ." Now my mother demanded I get into the elevator, but her commands went unheeded. "And God doesn't hate babies. God doesn't hate anyone. He even doesn't hate people who say mean things about others."

Now my mother grabbed my arm and pulled me away.

She didn't say a word all the way up to our sixth-floor apartment. She pointed to my bedroom door and I understood I was to go in there and stay. She didn't say anything the rest of the afternoon. I sat on my bed, and at my desk writing things in my little notebook, and then looking out the window watching cars ride by, a bus then another, and people rushing on the sidewalk eager to get from one place to another. They all held stories I wanted to know about.

I could smell a special dinner being prepared. My father had been away on business in Venezuela for the past week, so a big meal was very unusual. Finally, a few hours later I was called to supper. There, sitting at the table where my mother had set out a feast of lamb and potatoes and a green bean casserole, was Miss Harrison. Miss Harrison.

"I thought we could all use a little company tonight," my mom chirped in an unusually buoyant tone. I was delighted. We spent the entire dinner laughing and talking and sharing experiences about living in the city.

Later, when my mom came into my room to kiss me good night, I asked her why she invited Miss Harrison to dinner. "Because, Sylvia, you were right. You were right to use your voice to those women and you were right in what you said. I had to think a lot about it. I needed time to think. But, when there is a wrong and we can do something, we should try. Even if it's just," now she smiled and continued, "making a delicious dinner for a lonely, scared woman who is now our friend."

CHAPTER 22

KINDRED SPIRITS

"So what kind of chores can you do?" Miss Dennis asked me as we stood waiting for the elevator. It was 1961, I was eleven years old, and I had put up signs all over our apartment building offering to work for twenty-five cents an hour. "I'm pretty good with little kids, and I can follow directions . . ." And then I had a sudden wave of remorse remembering the terrible cooking incident last week where I started reading a book while a cake was in the oven and not until my mother came home to a smoke-filled kitchen did I realize I had not paid attention to the time. "Ummm . . . mostly. Sometimes I can get distracted," I replied.

"Are you saving for something in particular?" she asked.

Now I could answer quickly and earnestly. "Yes! I absolutely have to have my very own copy of a book. I read all the time and get all my books from the library. Miss Jones from the bookmobile always has good recommendations. But there's a book I've taken out so many times that it hurts me now to give it back. It's *Anne of Green Gables.* And I feel sad about that because I do want everyone else to read it too, but I want to have it with me. Right here in my hands." I sighed.

Miss Dennis smiled kindly. "Well, I think I might need someone to do some dusting. Would you be free on Saturday morning?" I was elated.

Miss Dennis's apartment, 5G, was one floor below ours so on Saturday morning my excitement wouldn't let me wait for the elevator and I just skipped down the stairs. When she answered the bell and led me into her living room, I gasped. "That is the most beautiful thing I've ever seen in an apartment," I said. "I am breathless with joy."

Miss Dennis laughed kindly. "Breathless with joy? Oh my, you do read a lot, don't you?"

But I was truly overcome. She had an entire wall of books. An entire wall. "Are those all yours? All of them?"

She nodded. "Yes, they are. And what I'd like you to do is dust them for me, please. And if you do a good job, I'd like you to come each week for an hour and dust them."

For the next two months I spent each Saturday morning with Miss Dennis. After I had finished my job, I always had questions about the titles, and that led to long discussions about things. One of the first things I learned was that Miss Dennis was thirty-five years old, a lawyer, not married, and not planning on getting married. "Well, I was engaged for a short while, but he wanted me to stop my career and I just couldn't," she told me one day. "I figured that if some-one didn't want me to do something that I really loved, how could I live with them knowing that they didn't really want the entire me?" I nodded, sort of understanding.

That's when the envelopes started.

A few days after our discussion I remembered a quote from my *Anne of Green Gables* book that reminded me of what she had said: "There's such a lot of different Annes in me. I sometimes think that is why I'm such a troublesome person. If I was just the one Anne it would be ever so much more comfortable, but then it wouldn't be half so interesting." I cop-ied it, put it in an envelope, and slid it under her door. On Thursday when I got home from school my amused mother told me she had found an envelope addressed to me slipped under the door. I giggled and ran into my room where I opened it ceremoniously. In it was a quote from a book I had never read but saw on Miss Dennis's shelf, *Jane Eyre*: "I am no bird; and no net ensnares me: I am a free human being with an independent will."

I thought long and hard about that. On Saturday I asked her about how independent she really felt.

"Now that's a difficult question, Sylvia. You know, when I decided to go to law school, it was a struggle. My parents just wanted me to be married like the daughters of all their friends, but I insisted I wanted to keep studying. I loved the law—the parsing out of phrases and the looking up of precedents and the sheer glory of constructing a clear, reasonable argument." She sighed and looked out the living room window at the sky.

"It's just wonderful. But my parents didn't understand—still don't—and were very angry. And then Jim, my fiancé, well, he didn't either. So I guess that even though so much told me I couldn't be a lawyer, I still had the will to do it."

"Like Jane Eyre," I quipped. And then I continued, "I think it's really confusing being a girl sometimes. I mean, on TV there are all those women who are moms, like on *Ozzie and Harriet*, and *Leave It to Beaver*, and *The Donna Reed Show*, and they always look perfect. None of them ever has, you know, a real job. And I think even my mom is confused. She wants me to have a career, she says, but says I need to get married too. She was going to be a doctor, but stopped to have me. And then it was really bad with her first husband but she really couldn't support herself. She wants me to not be dependent. But she also says I can't live by myself. It's too scary and too lonely."

Her phone rang, and I could tell by her motions that she needed to talk in private, and it was time for me to go.

On Monday her Jane Eyre envelope message said, "I remembered that the real world was wide, and that a varied field of hopes and fears, of sensations and excitements, awaited those who had the courage to go forth into its expanse, to seek real knowledge of life amidst its perils." I had to wait for the bookmobile to come back with my book so I could write the exact quote back to her. On Friday I slipped it under her door. From *Anne of Green Gables*: "They keep coming up new all the time—things to perplex you, you know. You settle one question and there's another right after. There are so many things to be thought over and decided when you're beginning to grow up. It keeps me busy all the time thinking them over and deciding what's right. It's a serious thing to grow up, isn't it?"

I had a few other chore-jobs as well, and at the end of two months I had exactly the right amount of money to buy my book. My parents found all of this amusing. They never encouraged or discouraged my reading, but actually buying books seemed quite frivolous to them. I had only had one book that was actually mine, a fairy tale book written in Spanish, given to me by a relative visiting from Argentina several years earlier. All others came from the library. But knowing my seriousness and resolve on this matter, my father took me on the subway and two buses to get to the big bookstore downtown, Brentano's. "You know, Sylvia, I'm quite proud of the way you set your mind on your goal and you worked very hard to achieve it. It's an admirable trait. I think it will serve you well in your future." And he took my hand in his, sitting on the cross-town bus, and said, "You will do good things in the world. Set your mind to it."

A panic set in as we neared the store. What if they didn't have it in stock? What if it was out of print? We walked through the big front doors and I marched right to the counter and set down my five dollars. "May I have a copy of *Anne of Green Gables*, please?" The clerk smiled, went downstairs to the storeroom, and came back with the most beautiful book I had ever seen. Then he wrapped it, put it in a bag, handed it to me, and I skipped out of the store.

That Saturday I took my book to show Miss Dennis. We both reveled in the nubby green cover, the gold lettering on the title, and the linen feel of the pages. "Your Anne is a really wonderful character, isn't she?" Miss Dennis said. "I'll bet she's able to do all of the things she sets her mind on. And you know all those television women you see on those shows? They act those parts. That's an actual job they have. In real life, they are hardworking women." I had not thought of this but it certainly made sense.

Her doorbell rang, and a tall, thin man with glasses stood there, awkwardly holding some flowers. "Hello, Harold, please come in. This is my friend Sylvia. We were just talking about women and our roles in the world."

Harold smiled, looked me in the eye, and said, "Women have a lot of prejudice to overcome, but why on earth would anyone want to hold back all of that power and possibility? Women can be anything at all. Anything."

Miss Dennis smiled. "Harold is a lawyer with the ACLU. He fights for equal rights for all." I decided I liked him.

The envelopes continued but I didn't see Miss Dennis very much. We both were involved in other things. For my part I had a thriving after-school babysitting business which helped me buy three more books and Miss Dennis had several big court cases and seemed to spend a lot of time with Harold. "I think he and I might start our own practice one day soon. So much to look forward to!" she told me in the elevator one day. My envelope to her that week from my Anne book had: "Oh, it's delightful to have ambitions. I'm so glad I have such a lot. And there never seems to be any end to them—that's the best of it. Just as soon as you attain one ambition you see another one glittering higher up still. It does make life so interesting."

A year later, in 1963, I was off at boarding school when

an envelope came in the mail. I recognized the writing immediately. In the center of a crisp white sheet of paper was the
quote from *Jane Eyre*: "Reader, I married him." And then
below, in her own words, "We are going, together, to Selma,
Alabama, to work for the civil rights movement. They need
lawyers."

JANE EYRE

The Original 1847 Edition With Complete Illustrations
(A Classic Illustrated Novel of Charlotte Brontë)

CHARLOTTE BRONTE

ANNE of
GREEN GABLES
By
L.M.MONTGOMERY

CHAPTER 23

THE GIFT

At eleven years old I saved and saved
To buy my father bright yellow socks
For Father's Day—
Mother warned me that he only wore black ones
"Don't be disappointed if he tosses them," she said—

I waited nervously for him to open my present

Although, looking back, I recognize the folly of my
    choice
(Expecting a businessman to wear yellow socks to Wall
    Street in 1961)
At the time he embraced me with delight.
"These are very colorful Sylvia—just like you," he said.
    "I'll wear them proudly!"

For many days he wore them out of the house
Every morning with his gray business suit

I learned years later that
He kept an extra pair of black ones in his briefcase
To change on the train to work and on the way home—
I imagine him bent over his feet with the clanking and
    twisting of the ride
Carefully moving yellow to black—black to yellow then
    tying wing-tip laces
Holding his balance carefully

CHAPTER 24

"AMOR VINCIT OMNIA" (LOVE CONQUERS ALL)—VIRGIL

We didn't see Mrs. O'Hara for weeks after her husband, Patrick, died. Before his sudden death, the entire building was full of gossip about him. "I heard him yelling until two in the morning," Mrs. Cohen volunteered when talk turned to stories about him, "and I heard crashing, like stuff was being thrown around." Then she'd point toward the ceiling reminding everyone that she lived right below the O'Haras and had direct access to details. "I've seen Patricia with red swollen eyes lots of days," Mrs. Jonas contributed, "and I ask if she's fine, and she always smiles sweetly and tells me she's fine. Just fine. Such a nice woman. She doesn't deserve all that unhappiness."

It was 1961, I was eleven, and we were living in Queens, New York City, in apartment 6L of our complex. I loved it there. Every day brought new interactions in the elevator or the lobby or the mailboxes or the benches by the front door. Sometimes I'd overhear stories that so captured my imagination I had to run up the six flights of stairs, race into my room, and write down the details so I wouldn't forget. Eventually I started walking around with a little notebook and a tiny pencil stashed in my pockets.

Mrs. Patricia O'Hara lived in 4N, which I learned when I helped her carry a particularly large box from the mailroom earlier that year. "Oh, it's from my family in County Clare, don't ye know," she stated in her slight Irish brogue as I set the awkward box down on her dining table. "It's my cousin Mattie that sent it to me. She's my only relative on me mother's side. The others all died as little children. In '39 when we told her we was movin' to America she cried for days and days and begged me not to go." She quickly cut the string on the box, releasing the crumpled brown paper enough to easily pry the sides. The top opened and Mrs. O'Hara peered in and then softly caressed the contents, repeating, "Oh me oh me oh me."

"What's in there?" I asked, intrigued.

She seemed startled by my voice—by someone else being in the room. "It's me dress. Me special dress," she softly whispered, holding up an elaborately embroidered costume. "And look here, it's the very shoes. Me soft shoes," she continued, taking black ballet-style slippers out and holding them in her hands. She sat down clutching the items.

"That's the most beautiful dress I've ever seen," I gushed as I stared at the gold and red designs. "When did you wear it?"

Mrs. O'Hara told me her story. She had been a young girl in a small village just outside of Galway, Ireland. "A traveling dance master came to teach us traditional dance. I was only twelve, but I fell in love with the dance right away. I think that's where my son, Johnny, gets his love." She looked down for a second and then continued. "He turns twenty-two tomorrow and lives in Manhattan now, with his . . . his . . . his friend."

I was surprised. "I never saw him," I stated bluntly. "How come?"

At first she didn't answer, but after a few seconds she straightened her back, clutched the dress to her chest tightly, and answered, "My husband won't allow him in the house. Calls him horrible names and just shut him out. Forbade me to ever see him again." This made no sense to me at all. None. She continued, "But I do anyway. I take two buses into Manhattan to see him and to watch him dance. He dances with a ballet company. Oh, he's so graceful and beautiful. Sometimes it looks like he flies through the air."

The clock on her sideboard began chiming telling us it was five o'clock and we both jumped up. "Oh me. I need to hide this under the bed before Patrick gets home," she mumbled as she shoved the costume and slippers back into the box. We said our goodbyes and I wandered back up to my apartment.

I asked my mother about this later that evening. She was clear. "Johnny O'Hara is a gay man—a homosexual. That means he is romantically involved with other men. And his father doesn't like anyone who is not just like himself. He thinks his son's life is immoral. Personally," she continued, "I think Mr. O'Hara is just plain wrong. And it's causing his wife and son a great deal of pain. He is simply an angry, angry bully." I agreed.

"I've been wondering, Mrs. O'Hara, did you keep dancing? Is that why you have the costume?" I asked her a few days later when I sat next to her on the front bench. She looked out at the parking lot in front of us as she told me the story of how she won lots of village dance competitions and at the age of eighteen was scheduled to go on stage in the city of Galway when her fiancé, Patrick, told her she was not allowed. He didn't think that it was right to be jumping about in front of others and wouldn't let her do it. "I was young," she said, "and I didn't know anything else, so I just did what he said. And when the next year, right after we were married, he said we were moving to America, I just packed my bags. We didn't know I was pregnant with Johnny then, but he was born just a few months after we arrived. He's been the light of my life." She got up as the mail truck arrived and I went off to the playground.

And then, several weeks later, after her husband's death, I asked a stranger opening her 4N mailbox, "Are you a friend of Mrs. O'Hara's, because I'm worried about her. It's been a long time since we've seen her."

The man smiled at me. "I'm her son, Johnny," he replied, "and you must be Sylvia. She told me about you."

I giggled and responded, "She told me about you too. She said you dance ballet and it's beautiful. She used to dance but she stopped. Maybe she should start again."

Johnny jumped up. "Of course. That's it," he said, "yes.

Will you come to see us at four this afternoon? I have a great idea," and dashed off up the stairs.

When I arrived at 4N that afternoon, a smiling Mrs. O'Hara hugged me, took my hand, and twirled me around. "Johnny and I are going to do some traditional Irish dances. We thought maybe you'd like to learn a few steps too."

This was a great idea, but I thought up a bigger one. That evening I went to Mrs. Cohen in 3N, Mrs. Jonas in 3A, Miss Donahue in 6B, and Mrs. Thompson in 2C and asked if they could meet us in the lobby the next day at 10 AM. I asked if they could gather some more people together. We were going to help Mrs. O'Hara.

And so it came to be that twenty women and girls gathered every day for a week to learn a few simple steps of Irish folk dancing from Johnny and Mrs. O'Hara. Every rehearsal ended with laughter and talk that sometimes lasted for hours. By Friday we were finally ready and I made up small notices and hung them in the elevator, by the mailboxes, and in the laundry room inviting everyone to the front parking lot at 6 PM on June 24th for a gala performance.

And even though the sun had not yet set, the building custodian turned on the bright spotlights. Mrs. Gleason in 1H opened her windows and readied her record player, and right on cue, with Irish music loudly playing, our motley crew danced behind and around the graceful, precise Johnny and Patricia O'Hara while our audience leaned out their windows or sat on their car hoods or stood on the sidewalk, all of them—all of them—gleefully clapping and keeping time.

I had made a medal out of a can lid and some ribbon

which I very ceremoniously gave a crying Mrs. O'Hara at the end of the event, declaring her the "Champion of Irish Dancing." Everyone cheered.

A few days later Johnny told me that his mom was moving to Manhattan to live with him and his friend, Steve.

"Are you and Steve married?" I asked.

An astonished Johnny answered, "No, I wish we were. But you know that's just not legal."

"Well, I answered, "that just seems stupid. If you love someone shouldn't you be able to get married?"

He laughed. "You are right. Maybe one day people will realize that. But probably not in my lifetime."

The photo arrived in early July 2011. It was a family portrait of a beaming Mrs. O'Hara at ninety-two, seated and dressed in a full, elaborately embroidered, traditional Irish costume, and Johnny and Steve, both seventy-two, on their wedding day, June 24th of that year, the very day the New York marriage equality act became law. All three were holding hands.

CHAPTER 25

LEARNING PEACE

"Vinnie, what's 'juvie'?" It was late September 1961, I was eleven years old and in the seventh grade at P.S. 63 Queens, NY. I was somehow impervious to the fact that there were a lot of boys who were involved in gangs and who were constantly in trouble with the police. But kids talked and it was clear on our concrete playground spaces who to avoid. I just didn't know why. So I listened and took mental notes that first day out for lunch break. "Sylvia, you know the kid who sits behind you? Well, he's fifteen years old, and been to juvie. Such a shame." And then the gaggle of plaid-skirted, ponytailed girls I was standing with shook their heads disparagingly.

I could see Vinnie on the other side of the playground, lean-ing one foot behind him balancing on the wire fence—black leather jacket opened to reveal a white T-shirt. His jet-black pompadour-styled hair slicked with so much Brylcreem that the shine captured my eye from far away.

We had been assigned seats alphabetically and Vinnie Laconda was right behind me, Sylvia Kuhner. Now, back in social studies class after lunch, Mrs. Rathburg assigned us a short writing about our family's heritage. "Just write one paragraph about where your family is from. And then we will share them."

This was hard for me. I raised my hand and asked, "Do you mean like me or my parents or my grandparents? How far back?"

She was visibly annoyed to be questioned on the very first day. Sighing, she answered, "Just whatever country your family came from."

I raised my hand again. "I'm not sure what you mean by family. I have had two dads and . . ." She cut me off and dismissed my questions by telling me to be quiet and just do the work. I sighed.

I did the best I could and when we were asked to read our paragraphs to one other person, I turned around to read to Vinnie. "Hey, kiddo, you know, you ask a lot of questions. You don't just take stuff off of anyone, do you?" he said.

I smiled. "I can't learn anything if I don't ask. I figure if someone doesn't answer then I'll find it out another way," I answered.

He smiled a broad, warm smile and said, "I think you're gonna be OK, kiddo."

A few days later in English class Mrs. Jansen had to leave quickly and unexpectedly in the middle of a grammar exercise. There had been talk that she was going to have a baby, but it was only rumor so far. Vinnie tapped me on the shoulder. "Kiddo, what's this word right here?" he said, pointing to the mimeographed sheet on his desk.

"It's 'precisely,'" I answered. He nodded. "Hey, Vinnie," I blurted out, "what's 'juvie'?"

He rocked back in his seat. "Whyja wanna know that?" So I told him what I'd heard. "Yeah, well, it's true. And 'juvie' is a kind of jail for kids who get in trouble with the law. It's really like hell." Then he smiled at me and said, "It's 'PRECISELY' like hell." And we both laughed just as Mrs. Jansen came back in.

Our relationship turned into a sort of distant friendship over the next month. When he'd see me giggling in the hallways or on the playground or stairs, he'd almost imperceptibly nod a greeting and I'd mirror that move.

But on Friday, October 20, his mood changed. He looked down at his feet continually and seemed not to notice anyone around him. He didn't nod on passing on the stairs after gym class. So in social studies, right before class started, I turned to ask him what was wrong. I saw his shiny black hair cascading downward as he stared at his desk. He didn't answer me. Class started.

I generally took the bus home. He walked. But this day he came right up to me while I was in line waiting to get on. My friends let out an audible gasp. I left the line and went over to the fence where he indicated. "Look, kiddo, I got problems and I need to figure it out. Went to see *West Side Story* the other day." Ah, yes, half the school went Wednesday just as this new movie was released and had been in a Jets/Sharks Gangs frenzy for two days. He continued, "I gotta know more about that story. I figure it didn't end well for anyone. I gotta know more."

"How about the library? They have all sorts of information," I ventured.

He shook his head. "Never been in one. Those places give me the creeps." I almost laughed at the idea of a guy in juvie being afraid of my almost spiritual sanctuary. But I earnestly told him that I was going to the Howard Beach Branch tomorrow—Saturday—morning and I could show him around. He smiled. "See you at ten, kiddo!" and slid down the sidewalk as I walked back to my bus line and the gaping mouths of my friends.

The next day Vinnie was there—right at ten. We sat at a table and talked for a little bit so I could see what he really needed to read about.

"Look, kiddo," he began while twisting one hand into the other. "See, my mom has eight other kids. My pop—well, he did things. Bad things to her. And when he started doing things . . ." now he looked down, unable to meet my gaze, and continued, "to my younger sisters, I couldn't take it no more. I just hauled out and hit him. Hit him hard in his face. His gut. His side. He fell all bloody, and when he got up he left and got the police. They put me in juvie for that. My mom pleaded but didn't do no good. By the time I got out—in August—he was gone."

I grabbed his fisted-up hands. "Vinnie. I think you're a sort of hero. Look, you were trying to save your family from pain and . . . awfulness." He lifted his head and said, "No. See, it was what I could do right there. It's all I know to do. Hit. Push. Be in charge. But that don't end well, do it? I mean, in the movie all that hurting between gangs, it don't end well. There's gotta be another way."

I nodded in understanding as he continued, "See, what I want is to be a plumber, like my grandad. He makes money and likes what he does. I don't think I ever heard him yell, ever. We're living with him and my grandma right now and I want to go into his business."

I nodded again. This made sense to me. He continued, "Problem is, I don't read good. I never really was in school long enough and it was too hard. Think you can teach me?"

He looked at me plaintively and I was momentarily stumped. Then I jumped up. "I don't know how to do that, but I know someone right here who does," I chirped as I walked over to get Miss O'Neil.

Miss O'Neil was one of the kindest and smartest people I knew. Any time I had trouble pronouncing one of my favorite words she would help. She showed me what a thesaurus was and the biggest dictionary I had ever seen was mine to use whenever I wanted to. Last week my word had been "perspicacious" and this week it was "tintinnabulation."

I quickly explained the situation as we glanced over at a squirming Vinnie sitting alone at the long wooden table fenced in by stacks of books. She brushed back some wisps of her bunned gray hair, adjusted her glasses, grabbed a book from the shelf behind her, and walked with me to her new student.

For the next hour I busied myself in books while the two of them sat side by side, heads bent over a book opened between them, conspiratorially.

Their sessions continued for months and whenever I'd see Miss O'Neil she would remark "what a delightful young man" Vinnie was.

In March, Vinnie passed me a note during English. I read what he had written in his own handwriting eagerly: "Miss Virginia Clayton O'Neil and Mr. Vincent Matheus Lacona would like to invite you to a special event at the Howard Beach Library this Saturday at 11 o'clock." I giggled and nodded a "yes" to him.

That Saturday, very ceremoniously, Vinnie read out a quote by Henry David Thoreau: "I learned this, at least, by my experiment: that if one advances confidently in the direction of his dreams, and endeavors to live the life which he has imagined, he will meet with a success unexpected in common hours."

And then he continued by reading some passages from what he declared to be his favorite book, *Great Expectations* by Charles Dickens. When I clapped with glee I was met with a glaring, disdainful stare from Mrs. Wilcox, the other librarian. But Miss O'Neil was also in the spirit of things and laughed with us.

At our eighth grade graduation his whole family—minus his long-absent father—came to see him. In the noisy confusion of the event, I met them quickly but long enough for his mother to give me a long hug and whisper "thank you" in my ear and hand me his photo. He stood by blushing.

Several years later, when I was away at college, studying to be a teacher, my mother called me in total confusion.
"We just had a terrible plumbing problem in the kitchen.
The man who fixed it saw our name on the door and asked
if we were your parents. When I told him we were he actually grabbed my hand and shook it, and told me that you had
helped him become the person he wanted to be and to tell you
that all of his brothers and sisters go to school regularly and
will continue until precisely—he wanted to be sure I used that
word—precisely they felt ready to go out into the world. And
then he refused to charge us anything. Sylvia, you need to
explain this. How on earth do you know this person?"

"He's a friend from long ago," I explained and smiled as I
remembered Vinnie's favorite quote from that Dickens book:
"Pause you who read this and think for a moment of the long
chain of iron or gold, of thorns or flowers, that would never
have bound you, but for the formation of the first link on one
memorable day."

CHAPTER 26

HAVING WORDS

"Aha. There you are. Sitting in my own heaven," Rose said, smiling. It was October 1961; I was eleven years old and cross-legged on the floor right in the middle of Rose's tiny room in the Brooklyn apartment she shared with her cousin. It was filled from floor to ceiling with books. Books upon books were piled on sagging shelves; books peeked out from under the bed; books lined the small closet; and books were stacked on a small table in the corner. I had never seen anything more wondrous.

We were making a courtesy visit to a very distant relative, Rose, who now that we had moved to New York City, lived no more than a few miles away. I was prompted by my parents of what not to talk about and of how to behave. "Do not talk about the past. She suffered greatly at the hands of the gestapo. They killed her husband and two sons. She was skin and bones when the camp was liberated. Don't talk to her about that. Only talk about nice things."

This put brakes on my mouth, but not on my brain. I had a lot of questions and when I found myself confined to the living room couch I knew I had to walk away or my words would tumble out. I wandered with the excuse of finding the bathroom but stumbled instead into Rose's room off of the narrow hallway. I was enchanted and lost all track of time. Then I heard footsteps and creaks from the old wooden floors. I looked up to see Rose's smiling face.

"So I guess you like it here," she said to me in her thick German accent. "Is good, no?" She smiled. Her wrinkled eighty-year-old hand reached high above me and pulled down a green-covered volume. "Here," she handed me the book, "you might like this one. But look at as many as you want." Her smile was gentle and full. I had not expected this at all.

"I don't understand," I blurted out—betrayed again, but not for the last time, by my questioning mind—"My parents said you had a hard life and lots of tragedy. But here you live surrounded by books. This looks like the best place in the whole world to me. It's beautiful."

She sat down and began, "When I was in the camp I had no books, nothing to read. We couldn't have paper so nothing to write on. At first I was so miserable. Every day brought tragedy and pain. And then I began telling myself stories and imagining books in my head. What would they be about? What would they say? And remembering flowers. All sorts of colorful flowers. And soon every morning instead of dreading the day I looked forward to the books in my mind—to reading my books.

"Much later, when we were liberated, a nice couple took me into their home to help rehabilitate me—I was so sick and weak. They were English and I spoke very little of their language but I learned quickly. You see, they had bookshelves in the house, filled with books, but all in English. So I learned. And when I was able to get a passage to New York—Ah! God Bless my cousin Hannah who arranged it all—I vowed that the first thing I was going to buy was a book. In English. A book."

I was entranced. "And you did, didn't you? You did! That's exactly what I would have done. Buy a book!" I exclaimed.

She laughed. "Yes. Just what I did after my very first week of work. I bought that book you're holding now. And every extra penny I could save went for books. And now, look," she swept her hand around the tiny room, "I have all the stories of the world right here. It's like a miracle. Books are small miracles you can carry in your hand." She paused, looked up at the shelves, sighed, and then continued, "Ah, I better go back to your parents. They must wonder where I am."

After she left I looked down at the volume in my hand, the first book she ever bought, and I opened to a random page. I still remember the last lines of that poem—a famous one by British poet William Wordsworth—which have stayed with me. He's remembering an image from his past that has nourished him for years. A simple image really—of daffodils. These lines remind me always of the inner life that we have if we just wake up with the intention of creating a new story, every single day. And of honoring all those stories that came before. And letting them spill over the shelves and under the beds and on the desks of our minds. All those places where beauty and dignity live.

Rose lived to be ninety-five years old and whenever I would visit we would hold hands and together recite this poem, almost like a prayer.

" . . . For oft when on my couch I lie
In vacant or in pensive mood,
They flash upon that inward eye
Which is the bliss of solitude,
And then my heart with pleasure fills,
And dances with the Daffodils."

CHAPTER 27

A STUDENT STORY: DAN

"Nice ride you got there—looks sort of happy," he said.
There was a chill in the wet dark gray sky which matched my mood perfectly. It had been a morning full of small but mounting frustrations. On a short break from errands I was leaning against my red pickup truck outside of the no-seating-allowed Starbucks looking down into my hot cup of coffee. "His name is Henry The Helper Truck," I volunteered as I raised my eyes.

And then: "You're Dr. Baer! Wow. It's been about twenty years. It's me, Dan M. from your English class." I recognized him instantly. The multiple scars across his face. The severely drooping left eye. His warm, uplifting smile. "You know, I never would have thought of you as a truck person," he chuckled, "but Henry here seems to fit you well."

I laughed. "He does, indeed. He seemed like a practical

solution to lots of our needs, but he's more than that. He seems to have lots of personality. Lots of . . ." And Dan jumped in: "Character. He has character."

We chatted amiably for a few minutes. Memories came. Forgotten details. "I'm a veterinarian now, in North Jersey. I'm here for a few days to check on my dad. My mom passed away a few years ago."

We both looked at each other, remembering. He had suffered near-fatal injuries during the first semester in my class. The family home went up in flames and he rushed back in to rescue his mom and younger sister who were passed out on the kitchen floor. The sister died in his arms.

He returned to school the following year. I remember the downcast head, the reluctance to respond to any discussion questions, the defeated indifference to his work at the beginning. And then the change. One day he showed me pictures of a dog his uncle had given him—a terrier he named "Moxie." Slowly at first and then with gathering speed Dan's demeanor changed. Eager to demonstrate his hard work, his hand went up immediately when I posed questions. His papers, once careless and superficial, became insightful and precise. And, for the first time, I began hearing him laugh—a deep, throaty laugh that softened the hard edges of the metal desks, beige-painted concrete walls, and whiteboards of our college classroom and beckoned others to join him.

And twenty years later, here he was, smiling at me as I leaned against Henry sipping my now lukewarm coffee. "You know," he said, "when we studied that sonnet by Shakespeare—the one that goes:

'When, in disgrace with fortune and men's eyes,
I all alone beweep my outcast state,
And trouble deaf heaven with my bootless cries,
And look upon myself and curse my fate'?

Well, it was like he was talking to me. I couldn't believe how he knew how I felt. It was a low point in my life and I didn't know how I'd ever get out of it."

He shook his head and I said, "Good ole Will certainly understood the universals of our humanity, didn't he?" We both chuckled.

Dan continued, "You asked us to think about what person or thing or being made us feel hope—made us feel happy just because they were in our lives. And it came to me immediately: Moxie. No matter what, she made me happy just knowing she was in my world."

Ah, yes, the end of that sonnet.

"You know when I finally had my own vet practice, I framed that sonnet and put it in the waiting areas. Sometimes people ask me about it, but usually they get it. They get how thinking about love—a person or a pet or a profession—can make you better—richer. Can turn any day around. I'll never forget you for bringing me that gift."

He sighed as his cell phone beeped—a text urging him to get to his father's bedside. Before we waved our good-byes, he stopped and began the last lines of the sonnet from memory. I joined in joyfully and loudly, our faces turned to the sky, right there, outside of the coffee shop, on a cold New Jersey morning—with Dan at the open door of his car, and me leaning on my little red truck, my minor irritations now forgotten:

> "Haply I think on thee, and then my state,
> (Like to the lark at break of day arising
> From sullen earth) sings hymns at heaven's gate;
> For thy sweet love remembered such wealth brings
> That then I scorn to change my state with kings."

CHAPTER 28

COVERS

"Oy, you're later than usual today, Sylvia. Is everything alright?" Bubbi Kravitz asked as she ushered me into her house. It was spring 1962, I was twelve years old, living in New York City, and getting ready to graduate from the eighth grade. Bubbi Kravitz was my friend Ruth's grandmother who lived with their family in what to me seemed a massive four-bedroom house three blocks from my apartment building. "I had to send Ruthie out to the store for some more potatoes, but you sit here with me while I fix the chicken," she said, directing me to a plastic-covered red metal kitchen chair. "So tell me," she continued, "where did you go after school?"

Lately I'd been going over to Ruthie's house to help her memorize a poem. My friend was great with numbers and with science, but poetry just baffled her. A requirement for graduation was to memorize a poem and she was having a terrible time with it. So, I tried to help. But today I was late. "It took longer at the allergist," I replied. "He said that I've become sensitive to some new stuff and I have to get an extra shot."

For two years I'd gone to the allergist for shots twice a week after school. The bus dropped me off right in front of the office, I'd get my shots, and wait for the required half hour before leaving. But today, because of the new shot, I had to wait a full hour.

"Oy vey," Bubbi Kravitz extolled, "at your age, so much you have to suffer! Shots! You must be miserable about that."

I shook my head. "No, not really. Dr. Horton tells me that bodies change all the time and now that I'm a little older, I'm getting different allergies that make my asthma worse. But it's a good thing they can help me. I hardly have bad attacks anymore."

I had gotten used to the needle jabs and found that I actually liked sitting in the waiting room. Sometimes I would talk to the others and sometimes I could just sit and read. Afterwards I'd take a slow walk home looking around at the buildings or sky and notice even the slightest change from the last time. And there were always changes. The sky was never the same two days in a row. And even the buildings were different—some curtains were now open and some closed, some laundry was hung out on balconies on sunny days, and sometimes great puffs of steam came out of vents from the laundry room dryers.

"So, you and Ruthie are memorizing poems, eh?" Bubbi asked with a smile. I nodded just as my friend came rushing in with a bag of potatoes clutched in her arms. As she dropped them onto the metal kitchen table, the bag opened, and they scattered all over the linoleum floor making loud thumping sounds. Bubbi shooed us out of the room as we giggled our way into the living room to practice. She had picked out "Stopping By Woods On A Snowy Evening" by Robert Frost.

"But I think this is a stupid poem," she said, throwing herself, with a dramatic flourish, onto the plastic-covered green velvet couch. "I mean how does this even SAY anything? He's just wandering about not getting work done. Even his horse is confused. He's just looking at snow. So what?"

Bubbi came into the room wiping her hands on her cherry-patterned apron. "What's all this I hear?" she asked. From my spot on the floor I explained Ruthie's position. "So tell me the poem then," Bubbi asked. Ruthie read it out. And then there was silence.

I jumped in, "See, I think he's really appreciating the world around him. He's busy and he spends a lot of time hurrying around, but he's understanding how beautiful the snow is that very moment. Things change—even the snow's going to melt one day—but it's important to just enjoy what's happening now."

Bubbi nodded, understanding, but Ruthie just rolled her eyes and sighed.

Two days later, after the allergist, I went over to Ruthie's house again. The big test was next week and she had to pass. Bubbi was waiting with some delicious cookies fresh from the oven. "It smells divine (my new favorite word) in here," I declared, walking into the house.

"So I've been thinking," Bubbi said, handing me a perfect almond-scented mandelbrot confection, "I think your Mr. Frost the poet has a point. We don't really take time to appreciate a lot. And things change . . ." She paused to look up at the wall with a big wedding picture on it. She pointed to it and continued, "That's me in 1920 on my wedding day. Ay, it was a beautiful dress and the day was perfect. And my Manny, oy vey he was handsome! But now," she paused and looked down at her hands, "now he's gone four years, and look, I'm an old woman."

I felt she was getting ready to say more but Ruthie burst into the room. "Sylvia! I think I got it. I think it's in my brain now."

I sat very carefully and uncomfortably on the plastic-encrusted couch waiting. And she recited it perfectly. Every single word. Finishing with the last two lines, "And miles to go before I sleep//And miles to go before I sleep." "Now what's yours?" she asked.

"Mine is 'The Oven Bird,'" I answered.

"Let's hear it then," Bubbi said. So I stood up, my legs sticking awkwardly to the plastic as I did so, and recited it. "Say those last two lines again, please, Sylvia," Bubbi asked imploringly.

And so I recited, "'The question that he frames in all but words// Is what to make of a diminished thing.'"

"I don't get it," Ruthie groaned, "it makes no sense. It's just a stupid bird."

I shook my head. "No, see, he's looking at all the changes

in the world and in everything and how things get sort of falling apart, and then what do you do about that?"

"Well, yeah," she responded, exasperated, "so what does
he tell you to do? I mean what good is a poem if it's not going
to give you answers?"

"But my dear granddaughter," Bubbi jumped in, "there is
no one right answer for everyone so he cannot tell you. We all
have to learn for ourselves." I nodded.

The next week after Ruthie and I passed our tests, we celebrated at her house. "Now we're almost high schoolers!" we
chanted, barreling into the house, arms linked. "Watch out,
world, we're coming!" we finished before dissolving into fits of
giggles and tossing ourselves onto the couch.

Suddenly we were overtaken with horror. Something was
wrong. Something was very wrong. Bubbi came into the room
and found us standing in front of the sofa gasping.

"It's velvet," Ruthie exclaimed, "and soft."

"Yes it is," Bubbi replied. "I took the covers off today, and
look at how beautiful the green is without that plastic on it.
See, I think we should enjoy it. Now. We should enjoy it now."

She sighed, sat down on the sofa, ran her hands over
the soft fabric, and continued. "I wanted to preserve the
furniture—keep it perfect forever. But you see, like Mr. Frost
says, you need to take time to just enjoy it. And I think that by
doing that it doesn't diminish it. Yes, it'll get old and maybe
the velvet will wear off in spots, but it will delight all of us. It
will be useful and lovely. And when it gets old it will be beautiful in its own way. Different, changed, but still itself."

I ran over and hugged her. "You see, girls," she continued, "we are all changing and learning. You need to embrace life and live it without the plastic covering it. You can't preserve life. It's always going to change. You fix and you adjust. But you can live it and enjoy it. Accept loss and fear and even grief, but then feel the velvet and embrace the joy of it."

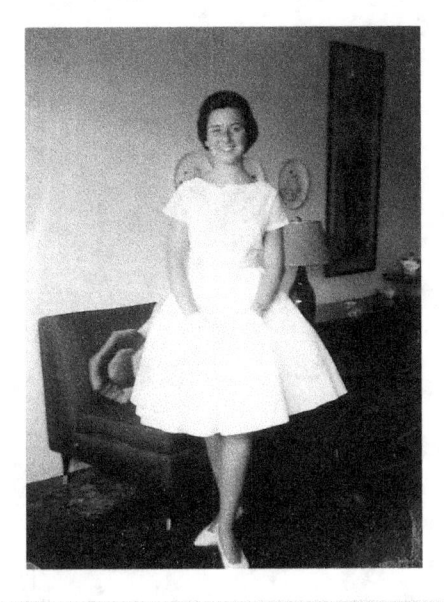

CHAPTER 29

FRUIT

"Remember the night I came home from babysitting the little Schwartz kids in apartment 5G and I had nasty scrapes on my knee and forehead?" I asked. "I think it was the spring of 1962. You and Abuela had been having another argument—I could hear you even when I got off the elevator down the hall."

It was 2002, I was fifty-two years old, and my seventy-eight-year-old mother was crumpled underneath a withering grapefruit tree in her Florida yard. Her crutches lying on the ground next to her, she had refused to move from that spot for over three hours.

She looked up at me with confused eyes that held terror in the corners—her mouth tightly stretched and clenched in defiance. I sat next to her and continued. "It was the night that I slid off their couch, hit my head on the coffee table, and fell on the bathroom floor getting a Band-Aid. I was a mess. I explained to you and Abuela that the Schwartzes had plastic covers all over their couch and chairs. Mrs. Schwartz had explained to me that they didn't want anything to stain them or anything to mar their perfection. They wanted to keep them 'pristine.' That was a new word for me, and I wrote it down right away. Little Jeremy spilled some milk on it right before I put him to bed, so I wiped it up with water. But it didn't dry. So a little later when I plopped down to watch TV, I slid."

Now my mother was more confused. "Why on earth are you remembering that now, Sylvia? So long ago! It's gone. Akkk . . . You and your stories. Don't you understand what I'm trying to do here? They are taking your father away. That's what they're doing. Taking him away." She started to shake and a volcanic burst of tears erupted and streamed down her face. I tried to hug her but she pushed me away. So I sat quietly next to her waiting.

My father had died three years earlier in 1999. Much of her life she had fought an undercurrent of sadness—depression—that her own mother had never understood nor had patience for. They were fundamentally different and I often became their intermediary trying to help them make peace with their opposing life-views. And now, with her mother and her husband dead, my mother felt she was without a ballast. She wanted to hold on to something tangible—some version of her own past life which she saw daily as leaving her—being ripped away and fading.

Tears now abating she said, "Your father planted this tree

164

when we bought the house thirty years ago. He cared for it and was so proud of having fresh grapefruit right in his yard. I never liked the stuff but he did and so did you. And now they want to take it away. I can't let them do that."

She was right. There had been a grapefruit blight in the county and all grapefruit trees had to be uprooted and burned to keep the spores from infecting the larger commercial crops. People relied on those for their livelihoods and their health. And, in truth, our tree was showing signs of sickness. For two days she had pleaded with the government workers who came and they had succumbed to her tears and grief, but also explained they would have no recourse. A crew was coming on Thursday.

I continued my story about the Schwartz couch. "So when I told you and Abuela about the plastic, Abuela was horrified. 'Why would anyone want to preserve something exactly like it was? Foolishness. Life makes stains. Sometimes it makes rips. Maybe you try to clean up and stitch, but those marks are what makes it real.' And you said to her, 'But it's never the same. The beautiful couch is gone. It's gone and becomes shabby.' And I remember trying to understand these two ideas."

We both looked up, startled to hear the whirring of electric saws and machinery just a few houses away. We knew what was coming. I continued, "Abuela said to us, 'Some people think that the past is gone once it's been lived, but I think that we keep adding. Nothing is subtracted from our lives. Even the difficulties become part of us—even those stains. And all of it leads us to where we are today. And today's embellishments and tears and scars—they add on to who we are. They all help us grow. It's all inside us leading us forward to tomorrow. It's not subtracting our lives—it's adding.'"

Now my mother nodded and said, "You know, I never really understood that thinking. I want to keep things like they were. Always. I wish I could cover my life in plastic. But the past is past and I can never get it back. Never." She started crying again and grabbed the trunk of the decaying tree, her tears rolling down its bark straight to the roots buried in the sandy earth.

When the men came, she allowed what she now saw as the inevitable—allowed them to help her up and into her house. I closed the curtains, as she directed, and put her favorite opera, *La Traviata*, into the worn cassette player.

After the men left, after the area was cleared, after the music had stopped, she and I sat at the table and had some tea. She looked at me, tired eyes swollen, shoulders hunched over her cup, body sunk into the fraying seat cushion, and asked, "So this story you were reminding me of . . . what do you think? What do you believe?"

This had been a question I pondered a lot. So many losses in my own life. So many stains on my body, my mind, my heart. So much past. And I answered, "I think that everything that has happened has made me, me. All of it. The past is never past. It's always part of who I am. How can you ever lose it when it's made marks all over your soul? And I think it's exactly that which gives life to learning and growing. Even if sometimes it means having some ugly stains. It's OK because it's who you are. And I think that remembering stories somehow helps us make the past and the present into the future."

She slowly looked up, smiled wistfully, and softly said, "So, remember the grapefruit tree in full bloom? Oh, how delicious was your father's smile when the first fruit came each year! He would rush into the house with a handful of round yellow globes—like he'd captured sunshine—and present them to me. A gift."

She sighed and patted my hand. "Maybe you have a point. I still don't know. Maybe . . ." she continued looking at the still closed curtains, "maybe, some day in the future you'll tell this story to someone, and it will help them take the plastic off of their own lives."

CHAPTER 30

FASTENERS

We walked to the elevator slowly, Mrs. Kovitz shuffling along, dragging her left leg, while I carried her one bag of groceries. It was 1962, I was twelve years old, and living in apartment 6L in New York.

"Ay, Sylvia, you're such a mensch. After taking the bus and subways, it's a wonder I can walk at all!" she said, chuckling between labored breaths and collapsing into her worn gray sofa in her apartment, 2F.

"Want me to put these away for you?" I asked, knowing the answer from the week before.

"Oy, yes, it's so hard for me these days. I don't know . . ." she said, shaking her head—sparse gray strands of hair barely moving.

I had known Mrs. Kovitz from the first day we moved into the building two years before. She had welcomed us by bringing a big batch of noodle kugel that tasted so much like my grandmother's that I almost cried. She saw my delighted eyes and smiled. From then on I would stop by her apartment for tea sometimes after school or we would sit on the big bench outside the building and talk.

She had no family. "Ay, it was a horror. No one left. My brother, my husband, my own little boy Moishe—all gone in the war," she told me one day. I asked her questions and she gave me answers. "They came to the house and put us in a bus and then a train. Like cattle. So many died on the way to the camps. I thought my heart would die when they pulled my sweet crying baby from my arms and threw him into another truck. 'Nutzlos'—useless—they yelled," she told me one day, her hands wringing on her aproned lap. "I had no tears left. I did what I was told. I could type and keep numbers, so each day I added and subtracted and kept lists for them. After the liberation an American family sponsored me. I was sick on the boat the whole time but when I saw that statue—you know the one, Sylvia?—the great lady holding the torch of freedom—that day I wept."

I loved our talks—sometimes about her life and sometimes about mine. "I'm collecting Green Stamps," I proclaimed one day.

"Ay, vas is that?" she asked in her still thick accent.

"You get these stamps in lots of stores after you buy things—according to how much you spend. And then you wet the backs of them and stick them into books. After you collect a whole bunch of books you can trade them for things," I explained.

Over the next year I collected stamps hoping to save for

a portable record player. "Each of those rectangles of green is like a piece of your life, isn't it?" she mused one day when I proudly showed her my second filled book. I nodded, delighted that she understood.

"Yes." Then I blurted, "My dad's business is not doing well right now and he's trying hard but we don't have money for things. So these is like a bonus in my life."

I began to see a real decline in Mrs. Kovitz's health. She spent almost one month in bed in February with only neighbors to take care of her. By April she barely left her apartment. I visited her when I could, and would often find her by her radio. "Oy, such stories I hear," she would tell me with animation and happiness in her voice, "what a miracle this machine is!" I would hear her talk about *Young Doctor Malone*, or what Rosemary Clooney and Bing Crosby said on their show as if all of these personalities were her friends.

In May I came home from school just as she was being placed in an ambulance. I dropped my book satchel and ran to the vehicle, banging on the closed door. "Where are you taking her?" I screamed over and over while my fists pummeled the metal.

The driver got out and opened the back for me briefly. "I'll be fine, Liebchen," she said with the oxygen mask pulled aside for that moment. And continued, "I can't manage on my own anymore. They are taking me to a facility . . ." The mask went back on and I was ushered away from the van.

"It's in Astoria," Mrs. Blandens told me two days later when I asked if she knew where Mrs. Kovitz was taken. I got the exact address and on Saturday I took two buses to get there.

Her room was clean but hard. She was in a bed with nothing but a window to entertain her. "My eyes are bad," she said, "so I can't read. Still, look, the whole world is outside that glass square," she said, trying to sound cheerful.

"Where is your radio?" I asked, suddenly aware of the sound of emptiness in that echoingly desolate room.

"We are not allowed anything that takes electricity here. So no radio." Her thin arms limp on the bright white sheets. The numbers tattooed at the camps suddenly starkly sharp against her almost translucent skin.

I left in despair, but the long ride home gave me time to hatch a plan. I knew what I had to do, and a lie was involved.

After school on Monday my mom went with me to the Green Stamps store. I plopped my canvas bag, heavy with filled books, on the counter. Having carefully studied the catalog I knew exactly what to get. The clerk smiled at me and rifled through the pages, making sure they were filled in thoroughly. He counted the books. I had exactly enough, having left the half-filled one at home. "What's your favorite song?" he asked, trying to make conversation while we waited for the runner to bring my item from the stockroom.

"Oh, I love Ricky Nelson! And his record, 'It's a Young World,' is just dreamy," I giggled while my mother smiled and shook her head.

He put my item in a bag and we headed home.

On Sunday my father—just back from an unsuccessful trip to Venezuela trying to launch his business there—drove my mom and me to visit Mrs. Kovitz.

"Look," I exclaimed, barely able to contain myself, "I got you something from the Green Stamp store!" And then I told a lie. It was a premeditated and carefully planned lie, but it was a lie. "When I went to get my record player I hadn't added correctly. I had too many books so I got this also!" And I handed her a brand new transistor radio, explaining, "You don't need electricity or anything—it just works all by itself." We turned it on and fiddled with the knobs until we found some stations.

Her face nearly burst with delight. As we left the room my mother clutched my hand and would not let go. My father was silent the whole way home. I thought maybe he disapproved of my lying, but instead he insisted on taking my picture the instant we got home.

Two weeks later Mrs. Kovitz died. The nurses called me and said she had left something for me that they would mail. I asked them, in return, if they would keep the radio for another patient who might need some happy moments.

The letter, transcribed by a nurse, came the following week: "My dear Liebchen Sylvia—I have carried this with me since the prison camps. When I do the numbers of my life— the adding, the subtracting—it seems I have nothing. But it's not a zero. I have memories and music and stories that I carry in my now failing heart. So I want you to have this, my young friend, to carry in your life. May it be a full one. And when you too are an old woman, may you pass this along to others so they remember life never comes to zero."

CHAPTER 31

DIGNITY

When I first heard the yelling it scared me, but now, two years later, I had grown accustomed to it, and, in truth, it had dwindled to about once every few weeks.

It was 1962, I was twelve years old and living on the sixth floor of an apartment building in Queens, New York City. Last year Mrs. Jarvis, just across the hall from us in 6J, had explained the situation one day on the way up from the basement laundry room. "You see," she began, "Mr. Cohen gets very angry with his wife. It doesn't take much to get him upset, and when he does he takes it all out on his wife, Muriel. Sometimes he . . ."

Mrs. Jarvis paused and clutched the rolling basket full of clean and freshly folded linens she had been pushing so tightly that her knuckles were as white as her sheets. She continued. "He strikes her. We've seen her face and arms with bruises.

Mr. Howard in 6N called the police once trying to help, but they said they couldn't interfere with a domestic matter."

It was a terrible situation. I talked about it with my friend Tony Nunzio from 6M, two doors down, who was almost my age. He didn't go to P.S. 63 like I did, but instead went to a Catholic school, Saint Theresa, a few blocks away. He loved the bookmobile almost as much as I did and when we heard it screeching down the block on Friday afternoons we would race each other down six flights of stairs to be the first in line. I usually won. We'd wait for each other to gather books then slowly make our way back home.

"I think somehow my dad is involved in the problem with Mr. Cohen," Tony told me one day on our slow walk home. He continued, "I'm not sure how but ever since my dad started working at their restaurant, Mr. Cohen's been angrier. He won't even look at me and one day in the elevator he said my whole family was a bunch of dirty Italians who didn't deserve to be alive. I didn't know what to do, Sylvia. I was sort of frozen. I couldn't even tell my parents because I didn't want to upset them any more."

Tony's family had been through a lot. His father came to the United States from a small, very poor village near Rome right after World War II ended, in 1945. Much of his family had died in the bombing even though they had never wanted to go to war, and those few who were left were hungry and tired and barely able to survive. But Mr. Nunzio, determined to have a better life, set off for America. He found steerage passage on a ship and begged his older sister Angelica to come with him, but she was determined to stay with her new husband, Vincente. "I heard my parents tell bad stories about him when they thought I wasn't listening. He has a bad temper and acts like Mr. Cohen," Tony told me.

Eventually Mr. Nunzio found good work at a restaurant, married sweet Mrs. Nunzio, and they had three boys and moved into our apartment building right before we did.

"Last year the letters started to come from Aunt Angelica," Tony began, "and now she was asking for help. Her daughter, my cousin Patricia, is thirteen. Vincente wouldn't let her learn how to read and when he found out Angelica was teaching her in secret he got real angry and started . . . doing things to her."

Now Tony hung his head and when he lifted it back up there were tears in his eyes. "Why are people like this to each other? It's so awful." He took a deep breath as we sat on a nearby bench, and he continued. "My mom and Mrs. Cohen were talking about this one day and how we could find the eight hundred dollars to pay for their plane ticket to New York. And Mrs. Cohen suggested Dad could maybe work part-time at their restaurant. They needed people to make extra knishes on Fridays and it would be a perfect solution."

I thought it sounded good also. Tony continued, "But Mr. Cohen said no because he didn't like Italians because he said they were stupid and dirty and nothing could make him hire my dad. But one day he was desperate and losing business, so he hired him to come twice a week. He's been paying him half of what he pays everyone else." Tony sighed and we both shook our heads. "Things are going to be different when we're older," he vowed. I agreed.

By January 1963, the yelling from down the hall stopped entirely. It quickly became known that Mr. Cohen was not well. In early February at the restaurant, right in the middle of screaming at a Chinese kitchen worker and calling him names, he had a stroke, collapsed onto his sparkling clean floor, and died.

We didn't see Mrs. Cohen for several weeks, although I caught glimpses of women from the building taking things into her apartment. I was curious and Mrs. Jarvis once more explained, "She's been through an awful lot and everyone is trying to help her in lots of ways. Did you know that now she's the owner of the restaurant? It turns out that she had been doing much of the office work for years before her husband died. But she's learning about more of the daily running of the business. She's learning to be strong."

My mother, who in her first marriage had her own share of suffering, was aware of what was going on. One day I saw her take an armload of clothes down the hall. "She asked me to help her get some more pulled together clothes for when she goes to her office at the restaurant next week. Now that she's in charge she wants to look more polished and she gave me money to spend on a new wardrobe," she told me, her eyes dancing with delight at having her own talent as a clothing expert realized and used.

In early June Tony excitedly told me that his aunt Angelica and his cousin Patricia were going to come from Rome to live in the U.S. the following week. "They'll learn English through a special program at our church and even live in the building across the street!" he gushed. I was delighted but needed to learn more details. "Well," Tony explained, "Mrs. Cohen hired my dad full time to help run everything in the kitchen and so his salary went way up. Plus, she paid him for all the work he had done that he didn't get full money for before. She said she was 'trying to right injustice one person at a time.' She wrote that down in her letter. So now we have enough money for the plane tickets."

"And what happened with Vincente?" I asked.

"Turns out that after their priest heard the whole story, he let Angelica and Patricia stay in a safe hiding spot in the basement of the church where there was a bomb shelter. They've been there for a week now right before their travels to here," he answered hurriedly. "I gotta go help because we're getting everything ready."

On June 8th they arrived. It had been a long flight but after they got off the plane at Idlewild Airport, the Nunzios brought them to their apartment, where there were great celebrations with knishes, and corned beef, and hot dogs, and spaghetti, and potato chips and cake. The entire sixth floor and many other building residents were there to welcome the newest additions to their American family with food and drink and laughter.

That evening after all had quieted down, my dad suggested we work on our family photo album. Every few weeks he and I would sort out some recent photographs and figure out where and how they would fit on the large rectangular pages of the album. We would place them in different configurations until one way just seemed right. My job was then to use a sponge to wet the triangular black corners and place them on the pictures. He would carefully pat them down.

While doing this we would often talk about all sorts of things. This time he was very specific. "So much has happened around here lately, hasn't it?" he began.

I nodded my head and laughed. "Well, Dad, that is an understatement! I can't believe how awful some people can be and how kind others are."

"True, life certainly isn't simple, is it?" he continued. "You've been through a lot yourself. And I'll bet that life will continue to surprise you and delight you and confuse you and anger you. But see these photos? Look at the one you took of your mom and me last week. See it?"

Now he pointed down to one of my favorite recent pictures. He said, "Do you remember what it took for that to come out the way you wanted it to?" I nodded and laughed as he continued, "You moved some magazines off the chair and tilted that lamp and closed the curtains. And when you couldn't move the couch, you asked for help to get it done. You worked hard to adjust things. People helped you. But when you look at the picture, it looks just the way you want it to."

I nodded, not quite sure what he was getting at, but he continued, "In life you need to adjust and move and redesign those things that don't fit. You have the power to do that by yourself and with help. You will create the picture. Your life will be right there within those black triangles. Make it matter. Make it yours."

are

VERS

for MOUNTING PHOTOS

DIRECTIONS

Slip a MOUNTIE on each corner of photo. Moisten glue and press on page.

FOR PERMANENT MOUNTING

Fold bottom flap forward, moisten flap, attach MOUNTIE, press together.

Popular Colors: Black, Red, White, Green, Gold, Silver.

PKGD. EXPRESSLY FOR F. W. WOOLWORTH CO...by

MOUNTIES, INC., BOSTON • MASS.

PAT. NO. 2,292,582   PRINTED IN U.S.A.

CHAPTER 32

A STUDENT STORY: JIMMY

The email this morning began, "Dr. Baer, this is Jimmy from your American Lit class a few years ago. I hope you still remember me."

Of course I remembered him. He was a friendly kid, always with a smile and a kind word. But college was not a good fit for him. I helped him the best I could during office hours and longer tutoring sessions. "I'm really trying, doc, but it just won't stick in there," he'd say, pointing to his head as I tried to explain essay structure. But I realized that he liked some of the readings we did. "I don't get some of what Emerson is saying in there, but I really like what he's sayin' to me about finding my own way. I think he's onto somethin' there. Like this quote right here," he continued, pointing to Emerson's words as he read aloud with a reverence I had not heard from him before, "'Nothing can bring you peace but yourself. Nothing can bring you peace but the triumph of principles.'" He smiled. "Yup. I get that. He's right."

I came to find out that Jimmy's family had abandoned him when he was five years old. His parents got divorced and his much older sister went with his mother and his older brother went with the father. Jimmy was left in the care of an abusive and drug-riddled uncle and aunt. And so at that young age he began to fashion his own life, taking and relishing whatever scraps of help and kindness came his way. Some helpful teachers in high school encouraged him to go on to college. Two part-time jobs helped him with the costs and he plunged into the academic world. But the hurdles were becoming too great. There was little time to do the necessary work for classes, do his jobs, and care for his now severely handicapped uncle. (His aunt had died of an overdose several years back.)

By the time he showed up in my sophomore-level literature class he was exhausted. But I never heard him complain. Never. He seemed to find whatever he could to be happy about—to enjoy. Life had given him so little, I thought, and yet he creates a halo of gladness around himself.

Throughout our semester he continued to read what he could and talk to me about some of his favorite parts. "See, doc, in *The Old Man and The Sea*, Santiago just does not give up, does he? I mean he's old and sort of sick and mostly alone, but he still wants to go out once again to try to catch that fish. He keeps going. Now that's what I call courage!" I agreed. At the end of the semester he told me that he'd been offered a full-time job at CVS stocking shelves. He was very proud of this. "It's full-time and I won't be able to go to school, but I think that's OK. School and me—we're not getting along so well right now." He chuckled as he shook his head. "I think I'm just barely passing most classes. But one day I'll get back to it. I just need to go out and do what I can. 'Member Janie (from the Zora Neale Hurston novel)? She had to go do what she had to do and eventually she got to be who she wanted to be. I've got to figure it out."

A few days after our last class he came to my office to give me a small box with a present of a candle. Such a sweet gesture and one I fully appreciated. Or so I thought. Today his email included an update: "My job has been going real well. I've been working a lot and I think I'm going to be manager of a store soon. Next few months I'm going to be doing a lot of overtime extra work cleaning up and sorting inventory as we get ready to give those vaccines. The pandemic has hit so many people so hard—I see them come into the store and their eyes look so tired and afraid. I'm proud to be part of helping people get better. I can't be a doctor or a pharmacist or a nurse, but I'm really proud to be helping people however I can. Remember that thing you said to us on our last day of class? I wrote a part of it down and kept it in my wallet all these years. It's in there now. You said, 'You can take many paths in your future, but whichever one you choose be sure it's one where your light can shine. One where you can use your own self to make the world better in any way you can. You may think you're only a small candle, but even the smallest of candles can light up the darkness.' You believed in me, doc. So I want you to know that while I stock shelves and clean up inventory, I'm shining my light."

His official grades don't reflect it, but I think Jimmy is one of our brightest students.

CHAPTER 33

GARDENS

"Hey—Sylvia, why are you hiding over there?" Mrs. Marcon asked. It was August 1962, I was twelve years old and huddled in a giant green wing chair, hiding behind an opened newspaper, in the far corner of our apartment building's lobby. "This isn't like you. What's the matter?" she asked as she sat down next to me in the twin green chair.

"I'm so upset," I began. Then continued, "Look at me. It's horrible. I made a terrible mistake, and I don't know what I'm going to do about it."

Slowly I lowered the news of the day which I was clutching and crimping in my hands to reveal very short and very curly hair. "I saved all my babysitting money to get a permanent. My mom told me not to do it, but I went after school anyway and now look at me. It's terrible. And it doesn't . . ."

By now I was just barely choking out the words. "It doesn't even look like me. What am I going to do?"

Mrs. Marcon sighed and as she reached over to pat my hand a big book fell from her lap onto the hard gray marble-like floor. We both looked down, startled by the noise, and I read the title, *Silent Spring*, as she quickly picked it up. "I know a little bit of how you feel, Sylvia," she said. "I've worked so hard to be a chemist. My whole life that's all I wanted to do and I've been lucky that my parents and then my husband helped me to do this." I nodded.

We all knew that Mr. and Mrs. Marcon in apartment 4G were our resident geniuses. Mr. Marcon worked for a company called IBM developing all sorts of systems. Once, on our short elevator ride together, he described that he was helping to create a way of computing that would revolutionize communication. "There's this system we developed called 'Fortran' and it's sort of a new language for machines. They'll be able to talk to each other," he told me while I held the elevator door open so I could ask him where this might all take us. "Well, we keep making mistakes but learning from them. Trial and error. And one day, Sylvia, we'll be able to be all over the world and type out information to each other instantly. Imagine how that will create wonderful things!" I was smitten with the possibilities.

Mrs. Marcon worked for a chemical company, and would some days come back from work with her white lab coat stained and her hair disheveled and a pencil, slide rule, and tissues sticking out of her pockets. "You know," I'd heard Mrs. Cohen say to Mrs. Harroway, after passing Mrs. Marcon in

the hallway, "that's just how geniuses are. And in their thir-
ties. Still no children. Well, what can you expect? And she's
rather ugly, isn't she?"

I disagreed. I thought everything about her was beautiful. One time when I saw her at the library she showed me
a chemical formula she was working on. "Isn't it just the
most beautiful thing you've ever seen?" she asked me, her
face glowing with the same pride I'd seen on new mothers
when they showed off their babies. In truth, I didn't understand any of what was in front of me, but I did understand
that in her language, chemistry, this was sheer poetry. That
I understood.

But now, we were both looking quite solemn in our green
chairs. She said, "See this book I'm reading? It's all about
how chemicals we've developed are causing a lot of damage
to our environment. DDT, for example. It's great for killing
all sorts of pests that kill crops, but it's also causing damage to
water sources which hurts wildlife which totally messes up the
balance of nature." By now she was emphasizing her words
by pounding the palm of her hand on the book's cover. She
continued, "And I'm helping the companies that make these
chemicals. I'm creating . . . poisons. I'm killing things I never
intended to hurt."

And that's when Mrs. Kurkowitz, who lived right there on
the ground floor in apartment 1C, found us when she came
out to get her mail. Each of us in turn explained our dilemmas
as she stood over us in her old housecoat, gray hair pushed
upwards into a cleanly rolled bun, sensible black orthopedic
shoes scuffed but clean. She nodded in understanding.

"OK, you two. Come with me, I need to show you something. We followed her into her apartment that smelled of delicious chicken soup and fresh bread. "Come back here to this room. Here." She ushered us into what was like an indoor garden. It was miraculous. "You see this? It's a new type of tomato plant. And, right there is a whole row of herbs. And over here are some beans I'm training up this sort of trellis here." One by one she showed us the plants jammed into the tiny room.

"You see," she continued, "when my Harvey and I decided we couldn't take care of a big house out in Huntington anymore we thought we'd get a nice little apartment and live quietly and be happy. So we moved here. But it was a mistake. I missed my gardens so much. Oh, I had beautiful roses and fruit trees and flowers there in Huntington. But not long after we moved, my Harvey got sick and he died." She stopped to walk over to a small table near the rosemary bush to pick up a photograph. "That's my Harvey. He was a wonderful man. But now here I was alone. No Harvey and no garden and a woman almost seventy years old by myself in an apartment that seemed like a mistake."

She continued, "So I decided that I would take where I was and what I had, and move on from that. First I had to think what it was that I wanted. What it was I needed. And what it was that I could actually do. I needed plants. I figured out that I could sleep in the living room and turn this corner room with all of these windows into a sort of greenhouse. I added lots of lights and brought in every one of these pots and plants and soil and started growing.

"You see," Mrs. Kurkowitz continued, first focusing her blue eyes on Mrs. Marcon and then on me, "we do what we think is best at the time. We make decisions that make sense. And sometimes we make mistakes. Maybe we don't realize the consequences or maybe we don't think about them enough. Either way, if a mistake is made, then what? So, I choose to see where I am and find ways of changing. Look," she said, sweeping her arm around the room, "my mistake ended up being a sort of Garden of Eden. A kind of brand new life." She snipped some rosemary and then some thyme and placed the sprigs in our hands. And continued, "While you have life, you have choices. If you make mistakes, start from there and change. Make new gardens."

We both left the apartment and silently entered the elevator and got off on our respective floors. My mother was horrified when she saw my hair, but I confidently explained that it would grow out and my mistake would be just a tiny blip in my world and even though it's called a "permanent" it's not. She nodded and agreed to help me style it with those new clip-on hair bows we had seen.

I saw Mrs. Marcon a few weeks later on our way into the building, my new pink bows bouncing in my lengthening brown curls. "I've gotten a new job," she told me cheerfully. "I'm working for the Food and Drug Administration in the city. We're going to be developing guidelines for healthy chemical uses for the environment. I hear talk that there might be a whole government agency to help protect our environment one day. I want to help make that happen."

And in the early 1970s she did.

A few years later when Mrs. Kurkowitz died, her children found packets of seeds in her apartment, carefully labeled with instructions for growing the individual plants. These were distributed to grandchildren and nieces and nephews— and me—to take with us into our shared future.

CHAPTER 34

IN CONCERT

"Oh, Liebchen, what are you doing here so early in the morning?" Mrs. Levitt asked kindly as she set her large basket of laundry on a nearby rickety table. It was August 1963, I was thirteen years old, and in the basement laundry room of our apartment building.

I had met Mr. and Mrs. Levitt in the lobby shortly after we moved in two years earlier. The large bundles they carried kept slipping from their arms, so I helped cart them to their apartment. It was a beautiful space with shiny wood furniture, comfortable plush seats, a big piano in the corner, and the smell of freshly baked bread in the air. After that day I would be invited to have tea and cakes with them regularly and learned intriguing stories of their times in Prague. I learned too about how they had been neighbors as children, imprisoned in the same concentration camp, and then reunited in

America several years later. "Such a miracle," they would both say about seeing each other in 1950 at a friend's house.

On the day Mrs. Levitt found me sitting on the concrete floor, my head bent down low, my hands covering my face, I was in despair. It was not quite 8 AM on a Sunday morning.

I looked up at her bright blue eyes, her round face, her softly curling gray-white hair, and almost burst out crying. "I'm completely without hope, Mrs. Levitt. It's useless to try," I began while slowly getting up from the floor. "I just can't sing."

"Achhhh," she sputtered, "nonsense. Of course you can sing. I heard you sing. Remember when we sang just last week? What was that song we both loved?"

I smiled. "'Getting to Know You,'" I answered, remembering one of my favorite songs from *The King and I* and how Mrs. Levitt and I laughed as we sang and dance-galloped around her apartment with such glee that after it was over we collapsed on her big red velvet couch in uncontrollable giggles.

"That's different. I'm going to boarding school in less than a month and look here, there's a choir and everybody is in it," I said, pointing to a page in the newly received introductory pamphlet I was clutching in my hand outlining all sorts of activities available at my future prep school. "And look, there are concerts. Concerts! Where the whole entire school participates. And they even make a record of it. I'm doomed, Mrs. Levitt," I extolled while dramatically collapsing in slow motion back onto the cold floor. I continued, "I've been down here for hours trying to practice where no one can hear me. But I don't sound any better at all."

"Let me put my wash in, "she said, "and we will go upstairs to talk to my Moishe. Maybe he has some good ideas for you." She quickly loaded the machine, put in carefully measured soap flakes, closed the cover, and inserted the twenty-five cents into the slot on top. The water started and we made our way out. "Such a marvelous invention—the washer machine is. Such a marvel. You put money in and it does all the work. And this too," she continued as we got on the elevator and she pressed the "4" button for her floor. "Ayy, such miracles in the world!" she sighed with a happy smile.

"Moishe," she called out when we got to 4C and she opened the door, "Sylvinka is here to visit. She has a problem." Mr. and Mrs. Levitt were the only people other than my adored grandfather whom I hadn't seen since we left Montevideo six years ago who called me "Sylvinka," a sweet Czechoslovakian term of endearment of my name. It comforted me to hear them say it. A thread from earlier times to now. Like Abuelo Meindl, they too were from just outside of Prague and were forced away from their homes at an early age.

"Ah, Sylvinka, what a delight to see you, my dear," Mr. Levitt said. He was a small-built man who always wore a white shirt, a tie, and a buttoned vest. His walk was carefully measured and he often had to hold onto things to keep his balance. The soft folds on his face crinkled together accordion-like whenever he smiled—which was often.

"She has a problem, Moishe, and maybe you can help," Mrs. Levitt explained as she busied herself in the kitchen.

I blurted out my despair and showed him my pamphlet. "You've heard me sing, Mr. Levitt, so you know I don't have a voice. I just don't have a voice." Until my last statement he had listened patiently, but at that he startled me by banging his fist on the side table and loudly proclaiming "Nesmysl" (nonsense). And then again.

And again.

Mrs. Levitt came out of the kitchen with a tray of pastries and some tea. And Mr. Levitt began, "Everyone has a voice. We use it for different things. Sometimes it sings loudly by itself and sometimes, sometimes it is best used together with other voices. You need to know what your voice is needed for. To tell stories? To entertain? To bring comfort? To bring joy? To remind others of the sun, the moon, the stars, the sea?" He wiped his eyes. I looked over, still startled, to see Mrs. Levitt also wiping her eyes.

And then she spoke. "During the war we were in a special camp. It was one that the Nazis showed off to make it look like they were being good to the Jews. Lots of art and music there. Moishe with his beautiful voice sang with other prisoners. The Nazis let him live because he could sing so beautifully. I had no such talent, but I could cook. Akkk, they loved my cooking. They brought people in pretending our camp was perfect—even the Red Cross came—and they showed off the musical talents of the orchestra, the singers. After the guests would leave, they would send away many of the prisoners. One day the best composer, he was taken. Another day more musicians. Killed—all killed in gas chambers."

She poured some tea while Mr. Levitt looked out the big living room window at some passing clouds and she continued, "My Moishe, he kept singing and then he started making up lyrics. Lyrics that said things that made the Nazis angry. Lyrics about justice and dignity and freedom. First he sang them himself. Then with others. I begged him to stop, but he kept singing—they all did. They sang in the camp and they sang on the trains when they were taken away." Now she stopped and bent her head.

Mr. Levitt turned to look at me and continued. "A small group of us, we escaped from the trains. They said it was impossible, but we did it. We almost starved in the woods. And fear almost killed us as well. But I kept singing and so the others joined me. Soon we were loud—we didn't even care who heard us. We sang for life." And then he smiled at me. "And what a miracle, Sylvinka, when the Yanks called out to us. We were so close to a base but they didn't hear when it was just me. It was all of us together that they heard. And they saved us. Saved us."

"So you see," he continued, looking right into my eyes, "a chorus is not about one person only. It's about all the voices together making a song bigger than any one of them."

I understood.

At my school that fall and for the next four years I was in the chorus. The sound of 600 voices in concert sent my spirit soaring to the sun, the clouds, the stars. One beautiful solo and then another punctuated our Vespers and Sacred Concert performances. But mostly it was the blended notes of individuals together—all of us transcending our earthly beings to something larger than we had the capacity to imagine.

Years later when my daughter was tiny, I would sing soft, gentle songs as she went to sleep. Then I made up lyrics as she grew and began to understand words. "Sing to me, Mommy," she would beg when tiredness or fretfulness was upon her, and my slightly off-key songs sounded beautiful to her spirit. But at age four, her own voice began to develop into the clear, precise, a cappella singer she would become. "You are my sunshine, my only sunshine, you make me happy, when skies are gray," I sang night after night, this our favorite song, first alone in my wobbly voice, and then slowly she began to join in.

Soon, together, mine blended with hers, and both of our voices sounded pitch perfect and beautiful and larger than either one of us.

CHAPTER 35

SWEARING

"Damn."

In shock, I dropped the large dictionary I was holding and with a loud bang, it hit the wood floor. I had never heard my father swear before. My mother did all the swearing in our family and vividly in both Spanish and English. But my father never did. So, on this day, September 2, 1963, while I was in my room carefully packing for my new adventure as a freshman at a New England boarding school, I was startled. My father was in the living room watching TV and as I ran in, I saw him cover his face with his hands. Then again, "Damn."

"Daddy," I said, "are you OK? What's happening?" I could hear the narration from the news reporter—NBC had a special event coverage of what they called "The American Revolution of 1963." I had heard about the racial tensions and extreme measures being employed against Black Americans; I had even seen what little coverage there was during the spring and summer about some of the riots of rebellion against this injustice. But now, it appeared this was a compilation of all of these major events. I sat down next to my dad as the end of the show was unfolding. Apparently throughout the hour-and-a-half documentary there had been an examination of the recent events, but underlying all of this was a questioning of why now? Why had so much turmoil happened now?

I sat silently as my father lowered his hands to reveal a red, tear-stained face as we heard Frank McGee's final words: ". . . that what was promised was not the White man's to give, as a father to a child, but theirs, by right of birth, as free and equal . . . parts of the nation feel the Negro is wrong and has no just cause for complaint, they're meeting force with force. And all these forces build and a revolution broke out in 1963 for the same reason that the earth on a given day begins to quake on an ancient fault line."

The show's credits ran with sad, haunting music in the background. I got up and turned off the TV. My father looked at me. I hadn't the word until later, when I recounted this in my journal, but he looked at me heartbroken. Heartbroken. "Why do people do this to each other?" he began. "It's wrong. So very wrong to judge others so harshly and act so cruelly. I would say 'inhumane' but humans are doing this to each other. Everywhere. Look at what happened to the Kim family last week."

I nodded. That was horrific. Mr. Kim, who lived in Korea, had worked with my dad for two years on an import-export deal. The business folded, but the two remained long-distance friends. Mr. Kim had recently married, and he brought his new wife to New York on their honeymoon. We were delighted to host them for an afternoon's jaunt to Rockaway Beach on a long finger of land poking out to the Atlantic Ocean, but right there in Queens, New York, a favorite place of mine. While Mr. Kim was taking a photo of his smiling new wife with my father and me, a small crowd of jeering men gathered. My mother, sitting on a nearby bench, grew anxious. The jeering, and now threatening, grew louder and the crowd had increased. They spit at us. Racial slurs against Asians which I heard for the first time were hurled like bombs, and threatening, air-jabbing fists punctuated the fierceness.

My mother had run to get the police, who quickly dispersed the crowd. As I wiped the hate-filled, spewed saliva from my shirt, my mother helped a now almost faint Mrs. Kim up from her crumpled spot on the boardwalk. My father and Mr. Kim were being questioned by the police.

We rode home in silence. Later, when they left, Mr. and Mrs. Kim thanked us for our kindness and my father, embarrassed by the event, apologized. Mr. Kim responded, "No need to explain. Hate lives in all countries. One day maybe it will die. We need to keep working on it." But they never came back. They never came back.

And now the race riots and the struggle, once again, and again, and again, for liberty and justice, there in our living room in Howard Beach, Queens, right there on our television screen. "Sylvia," my father finally said, "you have the good fortune of going to a wonderful school next week. Use that education—all of the education you have ahead of you—to bring understanding to the world. We need healing. Each generation needs to help more and more."

And so, yesterday, almost sixty years later, in a world literature class, I heard echoes from previous end-of-semester discussions. "Dr. Baer," one student began, "in *Gilgamesh* the ruler is such a vicious tyrant—only after his own power-hungry needs. He doesn't care about his people at all. You know, it was written more than five thousand years ago, but it's true today too. People still act horribly toward each other. So much killing. So much violence and inhumanity. Maybe it's just all hopeless."

"Ah," I replied, "but look at how Gilgamesh changed. What was it that made him return to his people a changed man? What was it that taught him humility and humanity?"

The class smiled—every single student smiled. And one young woman who seldom spoke, but whose papers were full of brilliance, who I knew to have difficult almost crippling circumstances at home, who was studying to become a teacher, burst out, "Love. It was the love of his friend that changed him. It was slow, but it did change him. We can make change happen. We just need to remember to love."

CHAPTER 36

RECIPE

When I answered the doorbell, I did not expect a nurse to be standing there. It was 1963, I was thirteen years old, and our family was living in Queens, New York, on the sixth floor of an apartment building. "Mrs. Kullenz wanted me to give you this," she explained, handing me an envelope. "She said you'd understand."

The nurse continued, "For the last week, I have been taking care of her down the hall in her home—last stages of cancer. Very bad. She died this morning but last night she made me promise you would get this."

I was stunned—I didn't even know she had been sick—and could barely eke out a "thank you" as she walked away, her white uniform rustling behind her. I stumbled to a nearby chair.

I had met Mrs. Kullenz in the elevator more than a year

earlier when some lemons fell out of her shopping bag and I helped retrieve them. Her old and wrinkled face smiled at me as she winked and in a very thick German accent said that a touch of their juice was the secret to a perfect applesauce. We laughed when we both got off on the same floor and she promised to share some of her cooking with me later that day. "It will be ready around three. Stop by then."

I was delighted to make a new friend and told my mother about it as I bounded into our living room.

"Sylvia, do you always have to charge into the house like that? And look at yourself, you are such a disaster again." This was something I heard often—my mother's annoyance at my appearance. Somehow, I could never look the part of her ideal daughter—clean, tidy, hair combed, socks perfectly aligned on un-scratched-up legs. She was right. I was a mess, but I couldn't seem to be different and my mother couldn't seem to stop being annoyed.

"Mom, I met a really nice older lady. She lives in apartment 6E and she invited me to have some applesauce with her later."

Again, my mother's resigned sigh of disapproval. "Sylvia, you always talk to everyone. Be more discreet. More refined. Young ladies don't just talk to everyone they meet in elevators. It's just not . . . dignified."

Later that day I wandered down the hall to 6E and began what was to be a long friendship with Mrs. Kullenz. Over the next year she told me stories of her childhood in Berlin and of her husband, a famous doctor, who died several years before WWII. Once she told me about her son who joined

Hitler's Nazi party against her pleading and begging. One day when her dearest friend, her next door neighbor Lisette, was dragged out of her home to be thrown into a truck bound for "the camps" and she saw her son's face in the driver's seat, she knew she had to leave.

"I did not know what to do. Germany was my home but I didn't recognize it anymore. The hate. The anger. The inhumanity. It was too much. So I packed what I could and my daughter and I took a ship to Canada where I had a second cousin who we lived with for a while. I worked as a cook for a nice family there. When they moved to New York, Karla and I came too. Two years ago I finally stopped. I was getting too old."

"Where is your daughter now?" I asked.

She took a deep breath. "She died five years ago. Car accident. Crossing the street to catch a bus a car ran into her. They told me she died instantly."

She looked away. How could I know at my young age the despair and sadness she had faced in her life? The disappointment and fear. She patted my arm. "So now the only one I have left to tell my grandmother's applesauce secrets to is you, Lieber Freund." And she did. We peeled, we cored, we cut, we added special ingredients to the bubbling mixture, and we waited while it cooled ever so slightly, all the while laughing and storytelling. "You see, Liebchen, how something so simple like an apple can bring people together?"

When the nurse came to our door my family and I had been at the beach for a week and had just gotten back. Right after lunch my mother was once again angry with me and I was getting ready to storm out when the doorbell rang and the nurse was there.

She left and I opened the envelope. There in Mrs. Kullenz's shaky handwriting was the recipe. I caught my breath and in tears ran out of the apartment and down the block to the grocery store, where I frantically bought a bag of apples, a lemon, and some other ingredients. When I got home, I made the applesauce. While I stirred, my mother came into the kitchen. We talked and I asked her about her childhood in Poland and about some of the relatives taken to concentration camps. She told me stories about her grandmother I had never heard before. We also laughed at some of the silly memories, and after the bubbling mixture cooled a bit, we ate.

"This is delicious!" my mother exclaimed. "You made the most delicious applesauce I've ever tasted." I smiled and glanced down at the paper with the shaky handwriting where at the top Mrs. Kullenz had written in English: "So you never forget how to bring people together."

CHAPTER 37

A STUDENT STORY: LAKSHMI

"We made these for you this morning," she said. "Please, please eat them now and tell me what you think."

Lakshmi was a twenty-year-old student in my Major American Writers course. She moved to the U.S. from India a few years ago with her family. Conditions there for her and her family were insufferable. English is her fourth language (three being different Indian dialects/languages). Every morning she gets up at three AM to help her mother, father, and older brother make bagels for their small shop here in a NJ town. She does this right before she comes to the college for her morning classes.

They have no car so she takes two buses to get here. After school it's two buses home to tend the store until late afternoon.

Somewhere in there she does her assignments for school.

I have worked with her a lot as I often do with students who need and want help and are willing to take the time to work hard. I have seen her blossom this semester from a scared and awkward writer to an eager reader and scholar as we traveled through Emerson, Dickinson, Twain, Hurston, Hemingway, and Kerouac.

She writes with confidence and poise now and uses words like "perspicacious" and "triangulation" and "curmudgeonly" gleefully. In short, she's become a capable and joyful student. Today (the ending of our semester) half an hour before the start of class she brought me a brown bag with some still-warm bagels and some tea. Ambrosia. The light but dense texture, the almost sweet taste, the aromatic tea hinting at some mint tones—all perfect for a cold, gray December morning.

When I expressed my delight, she teared up. "You have given me so much, Dr. Baer. America! What a wonderful country. Look at how much change it has gone through. Look at how important it's been to think about big issues in life. Look how—not without pain and effort—equality keeps being possible. Look—here I can go to college. It's a miracle."

She continued, "I wanted to do what I could to feed you something. Something. This is what I could do."

And that morning it was my student who nurtured me and who taught me all I need to know about life.

CHAPTER 38

PEACE BE WITH YOU

"Ooooh, these pizzelles are delicious! Such a delight. Thank you for getting these for us, Sylvia. That little Italian bakery only makes them once a year. Like them, Miriam?"

My grandmother and her lifelong friend were sitting at our dining room table. It was Christmas Eve 1964, I was 14, and my grandmother was visiting us from Argentina. Her friend, who had moved to New York with her grown children a few years ago, came for the afternoon. I spent most of the time in the adjacent living room pretending to read, but in reality the stories and laughter they shared was better than the book in front of me.

I made tea for them and my abuela asked if I'd run out to the Italian bakery for some pizzelles. "You know, Miriam," she said to her friend after I'd come back and we were all munching away, "Christmas is my favorite time of the year! The food, the lights, everybody singing, beautiful trees with decorations, and this drink—eggnog—that's so rich and creamy they put rum in it to thin it out."

"Oy, Malka, what a thing for a Jew to say!" Miriam scolded, trying hard to suppress her laughter. "If Moishe was alive, I'd tell him right away. And he would be delighted!" Now they both burst out into uncontrollable laughter, tears coming out of their eyes.

I didn't understand, so they told me.

My grandmother began: "Moishe lived on our block in Montevideo years ago. In Germany he had been studying to be a scientist. Oh, he was the smartest man anyone knew! Won awards that even came with money—scholarships. He never finished his degree because of Hitler's rules. His Christian friends helped him escape when the Nazis were sending university Jews to the camps and somehow Moishe ended up in Uruguay in our Jewish ghetto area with no money and no family and no job. He started helping Max Weiselberg the electrician, and soon became a wiz at it. Everyone wanted his help. He made good money, got married, and began his own family with a nice wife, Ruth."

Miriam jumped in, "The truth is that he was actually in love with your grandmother. Everyone knew it. But she couldn't get divorce papers from her horrible husband. Oh, that man was a monster. What he did! Oy, he was such a paskudnya—an evil man! The only good thing he did was leave. Leave. Left her and the two children—your mother and your uncle. So, Moishe would find excuses to come to your grandmother's house to fix things. I know she was in love with him too." A sigh came from across the table as a coy shrug found its way to my grandmother's shoulders.

Now, my abuela continued, "He married Ruth. I told him no I could not marry him many times. Women could not get a divorce and he married Ruth. I told him no too many times. They had two children and he was such a good father. Only wanted the best for his family. Always the best food he could find to nourish them."

Miriam chimed in, "And the best butcher in town, the one with the finest beef and lamb, was Louis Martinez. The problem was that Louis Martinez hated Jews and would not let them in his shop. We would have to get a go-between to buy the foods and it was so expensive. But if a Jew walked in Louis Martinez would hold up his cleaver and yell 'Get out, you pigs' so loud that it made everyone scared.

"But one day, in October, Moishe had had enough. The children were sick, Ruth was pregnant again with many difficulties, and he wanted the best lamb for shabbat (dinner) that week. So he went into Louis Martinez's shop (his friends waited outside) and yelled loudly: 'I need to talk to you, please.' Louis came over to him with his knife but Moishe did not back down. 'I need to ask you why you hate the Jews so much. We like your meats. You are the best at your job of anyone we know. We respect that. Why do you hate us?'"

My grandmother shook her head in disbelief as if this were happening right here, right now, and she continued the story. "So Moishe listened while Louis talked. He learned a lot about Catholicism which he came back to tell us and then every few days he'd go back and learn more and pretty soon some of his friends went with him. Louis Martinez learned a lot too. The Jewish prayers sounded a lot like Catholic ones. 'Wafers—we call it matzoh—and wine. We all pray over the same things,' they discovered."

She continued, "And we started buying the good meats from his shop. In early December Ruth went into labor. It was difficult from the start, but no one could believe it when she and the baby died. She was so young. And Moishe cried. For days he cried. I went to the butcher to buy some lamb and Louis asked why Moishe hadn't been around—he had a book for him to read. So I told him. You know, he looked genuinely sad. 'My wife died right after my son Samuel was born. Four years ago. It's terrible—the feeling of loneliness. Terrible,' he said. Then he asked for the address. 'How nice,' I thought, 'maybe he'll send a note. Or a flower.'"

She sighed, gazed out the window, and continued, "But no. On December 24th Louis Martinez and his young son showed up in our neighborhood and walked down the street with cooked lamb and pastries and vegetables bursting out of two big baskets. We were all out on the street to see this and followed him, like that pied piper story."

Now Miriam jumped in: "So your grandmother asked him why he was there. 'It's Christmas,' Louis began, 'and you know it's like our Catholic Passover Seder.' We were all shocked. He said the Jewish word 'seder.' He knew about Passover. Then he continued, 'Christ wanted the world to live in peace and for us to love one another. He didn't exclude anyone. Religion should bring people together, not make us afraid. If we don't learn from each other then all of Christ's teachings have gone to waste. Moishe helped me with this. I want my son and me to celebrate Christmas with him.'"

I was spellbound. Nothing I had read measured up to the intensity of this story.

Miriam continued, "'Wait,' Sarah yelled from her house, 'I have an idea.' Within minutes people brought chairs outside in the street. The baker brought out his bread, everyone found food in their pantries, refrigerators, larders, and set it all out on benches and makeshift tables. And there was so much wine! Moishe came out of his home with the two children and smiled for the first time in weeks.

"And we all had Christmas dinner together. First Moishe gave a blessing and then Louis Martinez said, 'May peace and love rule the earth forever.' And together, all of us, together we said, 'Amen.'"

Miriam and my grandmother smiled at this memory. My abuela continued: "Moishe died two years ago. His son is a doctor volunteering in Uganda right now—trying to cure disease. And his daughter had two babies and is married to a very nice man. He's not Jewish but everyone in the community loves him. It's Louis's son."

CHAPTER 39

INFINITIES

"Girls aren't supposed to be good at mathematics anyway, so don't worry about it. But have you been sure to brush your hair every night? Having it in a ponytail will cause it to break and that would look so unattractive."

It was February 1964, I was fourteen years old, a freshman at a New England boarding prep school, and my mother and I were having our weekly phone conversation. I was concerned about my algebra grades, but my mother pushed it aside. That subject was beyond the scope of feminine abilities by her calculations, and not one to be concerned about.

This had been her attitude all through my elementary school years. In truth, pre-computers or electronic devices, my basic computational skills were somewhat shabby. But I always loved playing with numbers and my father encouraged me. In 1959 when I was nine years old, and my parents and

I went on a long plane ride from New York to what would be our new home in San Paulo, Brazil, I suddenly declared nine to be my favorite number.

"Because of your age?" my mother asked.

"No," I responded. "Because of all the magic things it does." And I showed her a whole page crammed with numbers and calculations. She pushed it aside and told me to sit up straight. My father was intrigued and asked for explanations.

"Don't encourage her, Fred," my mother snapped before turning her face toward the passing clouds surrounding us.

"Look, Daddy, see, if you take any number and multiply it by nine and then add one by one across, and you keep it at one digit, you always end up with nine. Like this: 9x5=45 and 4+5=9. And you can even go way high like 9x4,532=40,788. Now, 4+0=4 then that 4+7=11 so add 1+1 and you get 2, now add that to the 8 and you get 10, 1+0=1, now add that to the last 8 and you get 9! See? It's magic."

He laughed delightedly so I kept showing him other properties of the number that happen when adding and then subtracting. "Well, you may have a few bumps when doing basic calculations, but you certainly have a big picture of mathematics. Arithmetic will be done by machines in the future, but mathematics is the bigger picture. And you have a really good brain for it, Sylvia," he said.

My mother harumphed and said, "As long as our numbers can add up to making rent payments and having food."

My father reassured her, "Sara, we have to dream. Look beyond the small pieces. Beyond the stumbling blocks. We have to look at all of it and not be afraid to make mistakes."

He took her hand. She yanked it away and continued looking out the window.

After both businesses in Brazil failed, we moved back to the United States.

I tended to stumble along in most of my math classes through the rest of elementary school and then high school and college, always looking for a more interesting way to solve an equation or measure a space. Using the ideas to write poems or stories.

At our kitchen table during a freshman year college winter break in 1967, my mother found me bent over my notebook, clutching a pencil and grumbling, and she asked what I was doing. "The whole notion of infinity is making me crazy. Our math professor explained that there can be more than one kind of infinity—multiple infinities—of different sizes. But how can that be? I'm trying to understand these equations, but they make no sense to me. And, anyway, if something is infinite, isn't it just forever? How can it be measured?" I plunked down my hand on the table with a force that surprised us both.

She sat down with an unusual weariness of spirit. My father had just moved us to a small coastal town in New Jersey to start a new business. He had grown tired of the city clamor and pollution and cost. He wanted, yet again, to start anew. Our finances were lean and I had to apply for a third loan to pay my college costs. She said, "I don't understand anything you're saying about numbers, but I think the human heart can feel different infinities." I looked at her, startled by the depth of emotion in her words, but had no chance to respond since at that very moment my father came through our front door with a big bunch of flowers. "Fred, we don't have money for those," my mother chided with her words, but her face could barely contain a smile.

"Sara," he said, "we need some beauty in our lives, don't we? What is the cost of joy?"

Years later, after so much life, in 1999 my father died. Month after month my mother grieved. She would not sort through his things. She would not box up his clothes. She would not allow the permanence of his death into her being.

And then one summer morning I found her in his study filling up a bag with his things. She was crying as she held the giant black trash bag full of clothes and papers and said, "Do you remember years ago when you talked about infinity?" I was astonished by this. It was so long ago and I thought she had dismissed that whole episode quickly—not having been interested, or so it seemed, at all. She now continued, "I think about infinity a lot. Not the mathematical kind at all, but the kind inside of our hearts. I think there's the infinity of pain that just doesn't ever stop." She handed me the bag and as I struggled to not let it slide through my hands she continued, "But love is a kind of heart infinity also, and I think it's a bigger one than grief and pain."

My father died exactly 8,471 days ago and my mother 6,665. Their arithmetic can be calculated, but for their distinct, multiple infinities in my heart there is no measure.

CHAPTER 40

FIRES

In truth it terrified me. In the 1960s, when my chore was to take the trash to the incinerator room, I was filled with dread. I'd walk halfway down the hall of our sixth floor New York City apartment to a closet-size room, go in, pull down the metal door, and insert the bagged trash. Sometimes I could hear it careening down the six stories to hit the bottom with a thud. Sometimes the smell of burning garbage would wrap around me and the whole little incinerator room. Sometimes I'd have to close my eyes and just not breathe because the smoke was so heavy.

Always, the idea that everything turned into ashes saddened me. My mother would say, "Sylvia, you are too romantic. This is life. It's only things. You can't save everything." She was more practical than I. I had boxes of photos and notes and letters squirreled away under my bed. By the time I was fourteen, a whole dresser in my room was taken up by my notebooks and writings. "We are going to have to get rid of all this nonsense," she would periodically tell me, sighing. "No," I would declare quite emphatically and continue, "All of this—this my . . . my . . . my life!" Often she would just shake her head and again comment on my romantic nature and wonder how on earth she had gotten a daughter like me.

In 1965, when at fifteen years old I came home from boarding school for spring break, things changed. My mother's mother, my abuela Margot, was visiting us from Uruguay. She spoke at least five languages, but English was not one of them, so all of our communication happened in Spanish. I loved having her with us. She slept in the other twin bed in my room and often we'd stay up late into the night talking. One time when I was quietly humming a hymn from our Protestant church services at school—my favorite hymn—she asked for the lyrics. So, I translated the English words into Spanish, "For the beauty of the earth, for the glories of the skies . . ." and continued, "Lord of all to thee we raise, this our hymn of grateful praise." "Now, that is lovely. A perfect sentiment," my very Jewish grandmother said, smiling and nodding approvingly.

She was lively and spunky and would tell me long colorful stories about her life and about people she had met. "Your mother doesn't like to hear about these things," she would tell me. "I don't know how I got a daughter so lacking in imagination like your mother," she would sigh. It was always clear to everyone that they were very different in almost all aspects.

Shouting matches filled with exasperation were a daily occurrence, and often I would have to intervene.

During one such event I was almost glad to leave their yelling and take trash to the incinerator room. But as I got closer, I could hear sobs—loud choking sobs of unbearable pain. I rushed to open the door to the closet-like room and there on the floor I found old Mrs. Shapiro crumpled on the ground in her very familiar large blue housecoat—the one with the all-over pattern of small birds in flight which I had complimented her on several times. "Ah," she would smile when we'd meet in the elevator going up to the same floor, "little birds help me fly." We'd both giggle.

But now, here she was in great agony. I noticed some small boxes around her on the floor and two large paper bags with edges of envelopes sticking out of the top which she had thrown herself over. I tried to understand her but her difficulty with English and thick Yiddish accent made it impossible.

I raced to our apartment, opened the door to the still hostile interactions, and yelled loudly, "Both of you. Stop. Come now. It's an emergency." Quickly they followed me. In Yiddish words I did not understand, my grandmother and mother learned bits of the problem. They helped her to our apartment and instructed me to gather all the things Mrs. Shapiro had left on the floor of the incinerator room. This surprised me, but I followed their directions and brought it all back.

Over the next few hours, through lots of translations, I learned what had happened. We all knew that Mrs. Shapiro and her daughter Emilia had survived the concentration camps by sewing. The German army's uniforms were in constant need of repair and the nimble fingers of the mother and daughter proved useful to them. Mr. Shapiro was an accountant and his use was in keeping close ledgers. We never knew of what. He would not say. When asked he'd shake his head in resignation.

After the war they were miraculously reunited and in 1950, when Emilia was twenty-three, they immigrated to America. She learned English quickly and began work as a secretary, Mr. Shapiro found work as a bookkeeper, and Mrs. Shapiro—still struggling with the new language—stayed home taking care of them all.

The rest, though, was new to us. We learned that the problems began four years later. Emilia fell in love. Charley was by anyone's measure a wonderful man—kind, considerate, generous, smart, witty, and with a good job as a new lawyer in a large successful firm. He and Emilia made a wonderful couple. All agreed. Except for Mr. Shapiro. He demanded they not see each other. Charley was Catholic and forbidden to Emilia. No amount of reason would dissuade him.

She married him despite this, hoping his mind would be changed. But he refused to see her ever again, and he forbid his wife to as well. Having no money or power of language on her own, Mrs. Shapiro was trapped. She would sneak calls to her daughter during the day and sometimes Emilia would meet her at a friend's house, out of sight. When Charley was transferred to Chicago in 1960, Mrs. Shapiro was in despair. One grandchild was born, then a second one. Emilia sent photos which her mother hungrily grabbed from the mailbox in the mornings and then stuffed into bags or boxes in the kitchen pantry—out of sight.

But on this day in 1965, Mr. Shapiro, on a quest to rid his apartment of mice, found the treasures behind the flour, the matzo meal, the gefilte fish jars, the salt, right there in front of him. Assaulting his temper. He yelled at his wife and angrily ordered her to burn it all. Burn all of it. "There should be no trace of that traitor in our world," he yelled out.

And so I found Mrs. Shapiro on the floor of the incinerator room.

My mother and grandmother planned. First they told her they would keep all of the items right there in our apartment and that she should tell Mr. Shapiro all items were gone. Over the next two weeks together they took her to the local high school where she could begin intensive English language courses. Then they contacted her daughter in Chicago and told her their plans. They involved Mrs. Daly from 3D—a social worker—to help with some new programs recently created for immigrants. Mr. Henderson from 2B—a hairdresser in Manhattan—began coaching her on some small hair and style changes.

I would come home from the library some afternoons and find several people chatting amiably, my mother and grandmother serving tea, and everyone—Mrs. Shapiro especially—laughing.

And then one day, Mrs. Shapiro did not come. My grandmother went to her door and heard loud screaming and, understanding the Yiddish Mr. Shapiro was yelling, she came back to tell us. "He found out. Somehow he found out." She and my mother looked at each other. No words were passed, but together they stood up. My grandmother grabbed one bag of Mrs. Shapiro's purloined treasures—my mother another one. I didn't understand but knew to grab a box and follow.

We marched, an army of three, to the Shapiros' apartment, where my grandmother banged on the door until Mr. Shapiro opened it. The only word I understood of her angry Yiddish lecture was "schmuck," a word I had been warned never to say because of how foul it was. But she said it over and over. She shook the bag in front of his eyes. She then grabbed a trembling Mrs. Shapiro by the arm and together we went back to our apartment, bags and box in hand.

I learned what my grandmother had told him: "You are no better than Hitler," she had said. "My religion teaches love and kindness. If you think you are following a religion that makes you hate anyone else, especially your own child, and makes you burn them, even symbolically, and shun them from your life—that's not a religion, that's a hell."

We called Emilia in Chicago and told her. The next day she and her mother were reunited in our apartment. They spent several nights in a hotel in Manhattan with Mrs. Shapiro's grandchildren, Jeffrey and Katrina. And with her loving and caring son-in-law. She learned his parents were unhappy with the union as well, and chose to spend time with their other four children and families instead.

A few days later Mrs. Shapiro, in a new pink flowered dress and a dainty pillbox hat, her hair done up in a stylish new shorter style which curled around her round face, each white-gloved hand clutching the hand of a grandchild, smiled as she bid us goodbye at LaGuardia Airport—off to live the next (as it turned out) twenty years with her family.

My grandmother was scheduled to leave for her home in Uruguay the following week and for the first time, during that full week, I saw her and my mother spend time talking— heads bent toward each other across the table or on the couch remembering some small or large event—laughing, crying together.

Mr. Shapiro was rarely seen. But just before he died of massive heart blockages and then attacks the following year (Mrs. Daly told me later) while I was away at school, as the medics were taking him out of his apartment on a stretcher, he maintained that religions should never mix and that he was right to uphold this. And then his heart stopped.

Each year for the rest of her life Mrs. Shapiro sent a few letters with photos addressed to my mother, my grandmother, and me, thanking us for helping her to keep her memories and also her future alive.

And my mother never again admonished me to clear out my photos and notebooks.

CHAPTER 41

DRIVEN

The elevator stopped its downward path on the fourth floor and five-year-old Victoria and her mom, Mrs. Wilson, got on. "I'm going to the playground with my mom," Victoria chirped, and continued, "You look angry, Sylvia. My dad looks angry a lot."

It was December 1966, I was sixteen years old and we were living in apartment 6L in New York City. The Wilsons were fairly new residents of the building but there were already rumors circulating. "She almost never leaves the building" and "For a young woman, she looks very tired. Doesn't get much sleep I guess" and "Do you see her arms? And her face? Something is going on there."

In truth I never quite understood the gossip, but I did notice that the Wilsons' car, parked in the space right next to ours, almost never moved. "Jim Wilson works in Manhattan and takes the subway," was the answer I got when I asked my folks. "And Dottie Wilson doesn't drive. Like I don't drive. You know women just make the worst drivers—can't keep control of such a large machine," my mother would add.

This was a problem in our house. My nervously inclined mother would not allow me to learn how to drive. My father argued with her—I argued with her—but she was stubbornly opposed. We tried to reason with her, but to no avail. She would not have it.

On that winter day in 1966 the argument had reached a fever pitch and I needed to get outside and cool off. Victoria could see it in my face in a short elevator ride. I walked to the playground with them and pushed her on the swings, went up and down on the see-saw, and slid quickly along the very cold metal slide—giggling all the way. Mrs. Wilson sat on a bench gazing out at the bare branches and pushing stray strands of her very red hair off of her face. A cold and bitter wind came up and we needed the warmth of being inside. Victoria grabbed one hand from each of us as we walked back to the building, but just in front of the big glass lobby doors she stopped. "Mom," she said anxiously, "is Daddy going to be home? Is he going to yell again?" A flustered Mrs. Wilson muttered something and tried to quickly change the subject.

In early January I went back to my beloved boarding prep school in Massachusetts to finish my senior year of high school.

During the winter and spring I made several trips back home but never saw the Wilsons. The rumors continued though, and now there were larger concerns. "Yes," my mother told me, "I saw Dottie in the laundry room just last week and she had bruises all over her arms and a black eye. Jane Dorson and I tried to talk to her, but she just shook her head and said there was nothing wrong. But something is terribly wrong. I know it."

My mother had had terrible experiences with her first husband. She knew.

After my June graduation I came home to quickly unpack before summer vacation. My second day at home I heard a loud banging on our door and my mother and I rushed to open it. Mrs. Wilson was shaking in front of us, her nose bleeding, her left arm holding a large shopping bag, and her right hand holding a crying Victoria. "Please, I need help," she sputtered. "Jim is out of control and . . ." Suddenly she collapsed in front of us.

My mother called an ambulance and sat on the floor holding her. I called Mrs. Dorson. She in turn gathered others to come and help. Mrs. Schmitt brought extra pillows and a blanket. Mrs. Thompson brought her granddaughter's toys for Victoria to play with. Miss Jensen, a nurse, came with bandages and supplies.

While my father and several other folks made a sort of convoy driving behind the ambulance to the hospital, Victoria stayed with me. I saw the shopping bag on the floor and looked inside. Mrs. Wilson had filled it with items for her daughter—coloring books and crayons, a change of clothes, her favorite toy dog. And a small notebook with some phone numbers.

"Who is Memaw?" I asked Victoria after seeing the name and a phone number in large print.

She answered, "That's my grandmother. She lives in Ohio. Mommy said we could go stay with her but she can't get there. It costs too much for a plane and Mommy can't drive." And while absentmindedly crayoning in a big "Tom and Jerry" coloring book she added, "My daddy gets real angry and hits Mommy, and yells a lot. Today he almost hit me too but Mommy got in the way."

I looked away, holding back angry tears, but now six-year-old Victoria looked right up at me and continued, "Mommy will never let bad things happen to me."

I called her grandmother, told her what was happening, and told her we would find a way to get her daughter and granddaughter to Ohio. Meanwhile, Jim Wilson was escorted out of the hospital twice by the police—once for screaming his right to see his wife without, in his words, "all those meddling nasty women being around" and once for knocking over trays in the hallway in anger. The third time his tirade landed him in jail.

Within two days Victoria and her mom were on a plane to Ohio, the plane tickets having been arranged by the women in the apartment building, Mrs. Howards insisting on donating the last ten dollars even though her meager pension was barely enough to keep the eighty-three-year-old widow in groceries.

The following week, my mother marched into the kitchen while my dad and I were quietly munching on our breakfasts and loudly declared, "I was wrong." My father put down his

New York Times, I closed my latest favorite book, *Pride and Prejudice*, and looked up at her. She continued, "Sylvia needs to learn how to drive. Now. She needs to be able to take care of herself and not feel that she's trapped. Ever." That last word she emphasized by pounding her fist on the table. And continued, "Why are we letting all of those 'bad women driver' jokes and stories take over who women are? Men tell those jokes and after hearing it over and over women believe them. But they're wrong. They are just wrong. We are capable, and strong, and reasonable." And with that she marched out of the room.

That afternoon I began studying the New York State driver's manual and my dad took me to an abandoned parking lot to start my training.

"Sylvia," he began before we turned on the ignition, "you have three important parts of the car: a rearview mirror to see what is behind you, a big windshield window in front of you to see what's coming up ahead, and a control station with a gas pedal and brake and a steering wheel for you to make your way right now between the past and the future. Hold on tightly and guide your movements."

He handed me the keys to start the engine and said, "You are now in control."

CHAPTER 42

A STUDENT STORY: ABIGAIL

Several years ago a young woman came to my office and introduced herself. "Hi. My name is Abigail Bretton and I'm a second-year law student at Rutgers."

She continued while dabbing her tear-filled eyes. "My grandma is dying—it's bad—it's liver cancer—and she keeps going through lots of boxes from her attic that I bring down for her. Yesterday she found this (she put a book down in front of me) and was happier than I've seen her in weeks. She told me I had to come here to meet you—to tell you I'm her granddaughter."

Now Abigail's crying had become more like sobs. "My grandma has been my rock. Somehow she managed to find money to supplement my scholarships to college and now law school. She said you'd explain." The title of the book? *Literature By and About Women.*

Oh, Abigail! I told her the story. Years before, her grand-mother, also Abigail, took a course I had created called "Women's Literature." She was about sixty at the time and was part of the older student auditing program. This was the first and only college course she had ever taken. Her writing was clear and witty and insightful. Her class comments were few but always brilliantly on-point.

One day, late in the semester, she saw me after class to tell me she would not be able to return. "You see," she said, "the beauty shop is closing." I didn't understand so she explained her situation: Her husband refused to let her go to college. She had wanted to go all her life, but he wouldn't hear of it. "Not the place for women," he would tell her. But he gave her grocery money and hair-do money every week, carefully doled out and handed to her as if it were a gift. She scrimped on groceries—buying lesser cuts of meat and being creative with stews and desserts. And she did her own hair, carefully washing it and setting it in tight curls each week.

Years went by but she had saved enough to start classes and she began with my Women's Literature course. After each class she would get in her car and spray her hair so that when she got home her husband would believe she had been to the salon. But when it closed, she couldn't keep up the fic-tion. It broke her heart to tell me all of this and she did so with tears, but also with determination. "I'll find a way to get this education," she said. "I will be back."

I never saw her again.

Young Abigail's eyes were wide with amazement. "I didn't know. No one knew. Now I understand this story. She said it changed her life." Abigail opened the big and very worn anthology she had put on my desk to a Mary Wilkins Freeman (19th century) short story entitled "The Revolt of Mother." "I need to read it again. And look at the notes she wrote on the side: 'A. will not have to struggle. I'll make sure.' I had just been born. I think that A. is me!" she said in a hushed, astonished whisper. I hugged her and sent her back to her grandmother with my copy of Emily Dickinson's poems. I highlighted a few pages. "This is for her. She'll understand. And later for you. You'll understand."

So, in the end, Abigail the grandmother, wanted me to see that yes, yes she did, in the only way available to her, by way of her granddaughter, come back to college—she wanted me to know her revolt was complete.

CHAPTER 43

WORTH

"Well, I didn't want to be here. Not at all. But my parents put their foot down, my brother insisted, and so I came. I was very unhappy. Maybe I still am," my great-aunt Liesel sighed.

It was 1967, I was seventeen, and heading off to college in a few days. My father's aunt had come to visit us at our beach house in Cape May for a few days. Now she lived in New York, but in 1931 she immigrated to the U.S. from Germany. My grandfather Kuhner felt a responsibility to take care of his youngest sister, even when she didn't want it.

We were in our living room with the late afternoon sun creating a sort of golden glow in our pastel-themed living room, and twinkling coyly inside her large glass of red wine. I was curled up on the right side of the large fading couch and she was sitting ankles crossed on a high-backed wing chair.

"Why did you come then, Aunt Liesel? I mean you were, what, in your early twenties? Why didn't you stay with your parents in Karlsruhe?"

She sighed again, took a long sip of the glistening wine, and replied. "You see, I had gone to Berlin. And there I . . ." She paused, looked out the window, and continued, "I had some adventures. Your grandfather, my brother, had been in the war (WWI) and set off against our parents' wishes to fight. He wanted to explore the world and even though he was only fifteen, he went. We had a picture taken in 1916 and sent it to the French prison camp where he was held."

I interrupted, "Oh, I have that photo, Grandpa gave it to me last year because I loved it so much."

We both smiled and she continued, "I was so jealous. I was seven and longed for some adventure. But I was a girl and my mother said I needed to learn to sew and to mend things. 'Women mend the broken and torn things in the world,' she told me. I hated it, but I had talent.

"My older sister, your Tante (aunt) Friedel, was cut out for domestic life. She wanted to get married and have a family and cook and keep house. I wanted to try new things. I was always getting into trouble." She smiled and took another sip of wine, then continued, "A few years after the war, in 1922, your grandfather came to America—again against our parents' wishes—to find a better future. He was going to marry Wilma and both sides were against the marriage. We were from the south of the country and she was from the north—near Dresden. It was not acceptable.

"So they left. They came to America. I so envied them. One day, when I was twenty, I don't know why, I got on a train. I ended up in Berlin. Oh, I had adventures there." She stopped again for a sip of the blood-red wine, and continued. "I met one man, he was much older, and so grand, who took me to the finest restaurants and cafes. I . . ." she stammered just slightly and continued, "I lived with him for a while. It was wonderful at first, but then he started calling me names. He had a temper and when he became even a little displeased he would yell. Then he hit me. Once. Twice. I didn't know what to do. I had no money of my own and I was afraid to go home."

By now I was entranced. I had always liked my aunt Liesel, but she really hadn't spoken to me much. Now she was talking to me as an adult. Telling me her life. But what I knew of her and what she was telling me didn't match up. But as I always knew, people have interesting stories. Lives are seldom what they seem at first glance.

She continued, "I wrote to my sister, who was married now, still living in our hometown, and happily had a baby on the way. She showed up the day after she got my letter, helped me gather my things, and go back home. My parents did not talk to me right away, but soon my mother explained I was to go to America to live with my brother. The conditions were getting worse and worse in Germany and they could not help me anymore. They were becoming very poor. Food was starting to be scarce and their clothing, I began to notice, was frayed and torn.

"In the weeks before I left I mended as much of my mother's and father's clothing as I could. Some nights I stayed up until morning, my fingers aching, my eyes burning, mending mending mending—like a penance almost."

She continued, "The morning before I left, my sister Friedel came to see me. She gave me a present—a beautiful white lace collar to put on my dresses. It was exquisite. 'But Friedel,' I said to her, 'this is so expensive and so elegant—you have no money for this.' And she looked at me and said, 'I have been saving a little at a time. Sometimes you need to have something you can see and touch to remind you that you're worthwhile. Yes, it should always come from inside of you, but when times are tough, we always need a reminder. Maybe we need to remember that someone loved us enough to give us that reminder. Never again let anyone harm you, Liesel, or make you feel worthless.'"

Aunt Liesel continued as the sun was slowly setting and the room was becoming dimmer. "So I came here to America and I lived for a while with your grandfather and Wilma and your father—oh, he was a difficult child and so mischievous—and then I married your Uncle Gus—such a quiet, steady man—and I got a job. At Bergdorf Goodman department store in New York City. I started out in the basement sewing hems and doing minor alterations on men's clothes. And then I was promoted to the lingerie department. I love it there."

"Aunt Liesel," I interrupted, "remember all of the scraps you used to give me when I was younger? I loved those boxes of fabrics you would bring as presents." Now she and I burst out laughing as we both reminisced how my mother expected me to make lovely little doll dresses but instead I made flags or blankets or streamers for my bike.

She said, "I've learned a lot working in that department. I fitted princesses and queens and Hollywood stars and even the wives of three presidents. And here's what I learned: We are all the same underneath. We all have lumps and bulges and skin that sags and wrinkles. We all have fears and needs and joys. 'Liesel,' one very blond and very famous actress once said to me, 'you know more secrets about me than both my husbands.' And she winked at me. You know, Sylvia, on my store uniform—my housecoat uniform—I always wear the collar my sister gave me. Always."

Now she stopped, set down her glass, and reached under her chair for a box I hadn't noticed before which she handed me. "You're going on a grand adventure soon. College will be full of new things and new people and new ideas. You have such opportunities now! So much to explore. But you, my dear niece, have no sister to give you a tangible reminder of your worth of your own power of how much value you bring to this world." And then with a twinkle in her eye, she handed me the box and said, "But you have your Aunt Liesel. I saved some money from my paychecks and bought you this from the grandest store in the world."

I opened the signature-colored lavender Bergdorf Goodman box. Inside a fluff of tissue paper was a new, beautiful, extravagant, blue and white slip, created by the very famous and trendy designer Pucci.

I was astonished. She took my hand and said, "If you ever doubt your worth or ever feel undeserving of a good life—whatever that might mean—look at this slip. Put it on underneath your clothes. And know that you are as worthy and powerful in your body as anyone else in the world."

I have it still.

CHAPTER 44

MRS. WALTER

"They'll be here soon, Mom," I yelled as loudly as I could. It was late June 1970. I was twenty years old and my mother and I had just a month ago been in a horrific accident. While walking on a sidewalk area near our home in Cape May, New Jersey, a car ran into us, pinning us and ramming us over and over against a brick wall. The severity of my mother's injuries caused her to have her left leg amputated and almost cost her her life. My own knees were broken and my legs severely damaged.

By July, after surgeries and casts and adjustments, both of us were back home—my mother confined to her bed upstairs, I confined to my bed downstairs. There was no in-home nursing care readily available nearby at the time since our tiny town was remote and somewhat isolated, and no resources to quickly find such help. Finally, we found Mrs. Walter in Port

Norris—about forty-five minutes away. But she had no car. So each day my father left at six in the morning to pick her up, and each afternoon he drove her home.

Some mornings my mother would wake before they arrived and, my own legs in casts and severely bruised, I was powerless to help her. The only phone lines that existed at the time were land lines and neither of us had phones available near our beds. So we yelled as loudly as we could. "The car, the car won't go away," she screamed. And I knew it was one of her waking nightmares.

Mrs. Walter was a small-framed, gentle, and mighty presence in our lives. A woman older than my parents with deep wrinkles on her face and permanent sagging bags under her eyes, she cared for my mother and saw to it that she began the required routines of movement. Sometimes I would hear her voice wafting down the stairs, firm and determined, as she recited, mantra-like, "Mrs. Kuhner, now listen to me, you can do more than you think you can. You will do this and I will help."

I was not a very different matter. Eagerly I moved my torso about as best I could but when I tried to engage my arm muscles a frozenness took me over. I knew that when one then the other cast came off, I'd have to support myself on crutches to regain mobility, but I seemed powerless. So I sat in bed all day and watched artificial life unfold before me on daytime television dramas. It was all I had—my eyes still unable to clearly focus on words in my beloved books.

By late July Mrs. Walter took me to task. "Now you look here, Sylvia," she began, "the casts are coming off in two weeks and I won't have you just lying here anymore. Look at you all skinny and pale. Like a ghost. You need fresh air and sunshine—like the plants."

I shook my head. "I don't know what's wrong. My arms just won't get going," I implored, head hung down.

"OK, now, honey," she said with a new resoluteness in her voice, "I'll hold my hands like this, and you try to push against them. Just a little bit to start." She put both hands up in front of me and my job was to push. The moment I tried, I burst out crying. It was a sob that came from some bottomless well—some unfathomably deep center I did not know existed.

She sat down next to me on the bed hugging me and rocking me babylike until I was able to regain my breath—my words. "Now tell me, what happened," she whispered. And suddenly I knew.

"When the car came at us, I tried pushing it away. I pushed, I pushed. I could hear Mom screaming and I tried to save her. But no matter how hard I pushed, nothing worked. I couldn't save her. I couldn't save her. I wasn't strong enough." Mrs. Walter handed me a glass of water and looked down at her hands.

"You know, child, there are so many things in life that we just can't control. My Billy and me saved our whole lives to buy an oyster farm. Used to be you could farm them in the water right outside our land—you had to rent the rights to it from the state and then you'd get all the oysters from your space and sell 'em. Oh, people were getting rich in those days. When we were married in . . . uhmmm . . . it was '40, we were both twenty years old and full of dreams. Folks from all over were buying all the oysters our area could produce. Billy and me worked in the processing plant and the buy-boats. Never had children so all our money was saved for the farm we were dreaming of. Right after the war, we had it. Bought it up in 1950—twenty years ago."

I was sitting up now and not even aware that she had been moving first my left arm and then my right in slow circle motions. "But you're working here now, what happened?" I asked.

She explained, "See in right about that time, early fifties, a disease took hold of the oyster population. Killed them. Contaminated the ones that didn't die. Oystering just stopped. Our farm was worthless and we had no money left." She stopped and turned her head to look out the small side window in my room where the afternoon sun was streaming in, and continued, "I knew I had to do something. I could either sit around and not face what happened and dwindle in misery, or I could look it in the eye and change things. I'd taken care of my mom and dad when they got sick and knew I could do that for other folks too. So I started doing it. Helping others brought me out of my own pain and helped me face it. And it brought in much needed money."

"What did Billy do?" I asked, expecting some grand redemption story about his life. But she shook her head.

"Well, he took to drinking. Never did nothing but feel the misery and the loss. He replayed it over and over in his head and would curse the bad luck. And one day when I was out caring for old Mr. Jasper in Mullica Hill, Billy drank a whole bottle of whiskey, left it sitting right there in the middle of the kitchen table, went out to the old oyster farm, and just drowned." Her shoulders seemed to hunch over just for a second and then she straightened up.

"You see, Sylvia," she said shaking a finger at me, "so much of life you can't control. Call it what you want: fate, God, luck. It happens. You tried to push the car away. Of course you couldn't control a machine that size and of course you couldn't control the driver's reaction. Impossible. But you can control what you do next."

Now she put up her hands again, urging me to push against them, and said, "You've got to learn that what you can do is find ways of facing the bad, wailing over it, and then getting on with your life. Finding the power inside yourself to do what it is you can do, and then doing it."

We heard my mother calling and with a quick hug Mrs. Walter disappeared up the stairs. She came back down to find my hands firmly planted beside me, trying to use my arms to push up my torso on my own. I practiced several times a day—over and over—getting stronger each time—readying my arms for the job of supporting me on crutches. A few days before my casts came off I was surprised to hear thumping on the stairs and words of encouragement from Mrs. Walter. And then, for the first time in two months, I saw my mother—she was sitting on one step and then another, making her way down the stairs sitting down, sliding slightly, one hand on the railing and the other supporting herself on the risers.

Make-up on, hair done up, wearing her favorite blue and white dress, she smiled broadly at me. "Look what I'm learning to do," she proclaimed delightedly. And continued, "I have decided to rejoin life. And this is what I have to do," she said, pointing at her awkward situation on the stairs.

When my father came home that afternoon he found my mother sitting on my bed, Mrs. Walter in a big chair nearby, and all of us drinking tea and laughing uproariously about some small silliness.

"What is happening here?" he asked in astonishment and uncontained joy.

And even knowing all of the hard work ahead of us, my mother declared as in a benediction, "We've decided to live the life we have," as we all ceremoniously lifted our cups to the sky.

CHAPTER 45

PIECES

"Trash. Nothin' but trash. Shouldn't of let those types in," the thirteen-year-old sandy-haired boy yelled out loudly as the school bell sounded for the start of the day.

It was 1972 and I had just moved to a small town on the Eastern Shore of Maryland and was beginning my second year of teaching. Except in legal terms it was still a very racially segregated town. School integration wasn't fully implemented yet and one of my classes was totally made up of black kids—mostly boys—that I taught in a large trailer behind the regular brick-and-mortar school building.

My students averaged about a second-grade reading level. The black school they had been attending got the books the white school was throwing out and it was terribly understaffed and overcrowded. Now they were in my classroom with new books, only fifteen kids, and a little white woman whom they called "Miss" to teach them writing, reading, and history.

After a somewhat rough start, I figured something out: the families felt they couldn't come to the school, so for teacher conferences I went to their houses. The first house I visited to talk about their really brilliant but distracted kid was a tiny shack on the edge of a dirt road. The grandmother greeted me with a sweet potato pie and some sweet tea. She was old and bent over and had the kindest smile I have ever seen. We talked about her grandson but then I asked her about her life. I saw quilts everywhere stacked in the corners, piled on the floor.

She told me: "I taken them scraps from all the clothes I made for folks over the years. They put to good use here. My grandmom showed me how. She was owned by the Mathers. She was but a little thing when the family was all set free, but that didn't change much of nothing. My brother was hanged and then burned cause he up and sat in the whites' park. My husband he got beat by angry men cause he tried going into the store to buy some fruit for his son—he went in the wrong door. It's been a long road and I want my grandson to do better. He got more chances now. And look, he got you."

I was stunned. How, I asked her, was she able to live her life and still smile—still make all those quilts? "You see, I take scraps that come my way and I make something that can keep people warm and that's pretty too. You see, Miss, hate ain't gonna get you nowhere 'cept dead—dead on the outside or dead on the inside. You gotta get the attitude of change and justice to get the world right with itself. And you gotta work towards the light of love. Go towards that light of love."

Her grandson became a heart surgeon in Virginia twenty years later.

CHAPTER 46

BRILLIANCE

"Large skirts were good for hiding books." My grandmother giggled as she told me this, and continued in Spanish: "La sociededad de mujeres intelectuales y brillantes." I translated quickly in my head—"The society of intellectual and brilliant women." Aha. I smiled as I looked at the picture she put in front of us on the table. It was 1974, I was twenty-four years old, and my abuela was visiting me for a week. She had come from across the ocean to my home in Maryland where I was embarking on my adult life, having just gotten married, bought a home, started my teaching career, and begun my (first) master's degree.

Spanish was the language we communicated in, but it was her fifth language. As a young girl in Lomza, Poland, she spoke Polish, German, and Russian. She told me, "We never knew which language we might need. First one army invaded, then another. We learned to listen and speak what they were speaking. It kept us safer. French, too. Yes. I learned the language of fashion and hats when I was young. Oh, that was a musical language." After she emigrated to Uruguay in 1930, she quickly learned the native language, Spanish. "You know," she said, "my name in Polish is Malka, but when I started my women's hat-making shop in Montevideo, I changed my name to Margot. So much lovelier a sound. I love the sound of words," and she sighed happily as she sipped her Earl Grey out of my new Wedgewood teacup—the Volendam pattern with a singing bird on a branch by its nest poised to take flight.

She had brought some essentials for our visit: good sewing needles of various sizes, a collection of very old buttons, and some photographs. Today she showed me this picture, from 1916, of a gathering of young women. "You see, women were not thought to have very much in the way of brains for higher thought. Ha! How small-minded those men were— some women too. Maybe they were afraid of changing the way things always were. We didn't have access to libraries or lectures. But some of us were determined to hear the big ideas of the world.

"Our town was so small (on the far northeastern border of Russia), but our minds—they were big and they were hungry. We girls got together to talk. Our fathers thought we were discussing food or sewing, but some of our mothers knew the truth. Do you see her?" she said, pointing to the girl in the far-left chair in the photo, "her father was a doctor. When her mother cleaned his library bookshelves, she would take out books—one a time so as not to create suspicion—and leave them on the floor near the door. Annika—who was prohibited from setting foot in that room—would walk by, put the book under her skirt, and bring it to our meetings.

"One time Greta—the girl with the tie standing up—paid a young peasant boy to go into the library and steal a book (a Martin Buber book!) because we were so desperate to read those ideas." She paused to nibble on the chocolate chip cookies I had baked that morning.

I knew that her father wouldn't let her go to the university, and that she made money modeling hats in fine stores which she used to pay her way so she could secretly earn a degree as a pharmacist. ("No one knew I was a Jew. They would not have allowed me in. Hard enough I was a woman!") But I had never heard of her life before that.

"You know, Abuela," I said to her as the sun shone through the big picture window of my living room, "even now in 1974 they tell me that women should not worry about getting higher degrees—being doctors or lawyers or philosophers or college professors. When I graduated from high school the best universities didn't allow women to enter. Even now it's such a small number." I slumped lower into the couch beside her.

"Look at this picture," she said, almost violently pointing. "Look. You see these girls? We got together. We found a way. We began. See Elza there?" She pointed to the girl with her chin resting on her hand. "She learned Morse code and helped get Jews out of our town in 1935 by tapping on walls and floors. She lives in Israel today and works as a translator. And Ada, sitting with her hand on her temple, she dressed

271

as a German soldier in 1939 and led twenty-five children to safety. Then she became an artist." She smiled and looked at the picture again. "And that's me," she said, pointing to the slim girl on the far right leaning on the cabinet. "I'm going to be the first one of this group with a granddaughter who will get a doctorate degree."

I laughed and said, "Abuela, I'm only just beginning a master's degree. I don't know if I can go that far."

She put down her cup, grabbed me by the shoulders, and looked me squarely in the eye. "Yes you will. There are always people who are afraid of change—who are afraid to lose power over others. Those people are so small in their thinking. So small. They might hold temporary power over bodies or lands, but not over minds and hearts. If we all just let the bright stars inside every human being shine—all of us have shining lights inside—if we could find a way, then how much better the world could be. That is what real power would be. That would make the whole world brilliant. However you can—however every single person can—we must all work to help lights shine."

Thirteen years later, eleven years after she died, I framed my newly earned degree in gold.

CHAPTER 47

TAKE CARE

She held my hand as I lay in bed dazed and in pain. It was 1976, I was twenty-six, and on what was called "The Women's Floor" of Easton Memorial Hospital in Maryland, recovering from my third surgery in two years. Ellen had the other bed in the room. Yesterday, through the fog of a post-operative sleep, I had heard bits of conversation from the other side of the sliding fabric curtain between our beds.

In truth, it wasn't talking—it was a man yelling. I heard his voice bark out loudly, "You can't do this to me," and "No, it will not be the same." It sounded like a television was left on and the overwhelming sensation of needing to sleep engulfed me before I could make any sense of it. But now, this morning as I woke up, she was holding my hand. "You were crying in your sleep, honey," she said, "so I thought I'd keep you company."

We talked. I told her about my severe endometriosis and the surgeries they had to perform to remove cysts and scar tissue. My body had turned against itself and connected my entire reproductive system by what the doctor called "spider threads—webs." The pain was excruciating. "So, what are you here for?" I asked her.

She looked down. "Breast cancer—the lump I had was cancer. And now they're saying my best option is to remove the breast."

She sighed and looked down toward the floor, her soft blue hospital gown gently floating over her body as she smoothed it on her chest, her legs. We were silent. Suddenly, a man full of jittery, awkward, jabbing motions burst through the door. His anger filled the small space instantly. Even the gray suit he was wearing seemed to annoy his skin.

"Henry," Ellen politely and calmly said, "this is my roommate, Sylvia. Sylvia, this is my husband." He barely acknowledged me before grabbing her arm, pulling the curtain between us, and loudly yelling.

Now I could hear him clearly: "If you go through with this nonsense I will leave you. You won't be a real woman anymore and I won't stand the sight of you. And you'll be lost without me. You are nothing without me." And then in a gray whirl he left the room.

I heard her crying. Slowly I slid from my bed and went to her side. "What is happening, Ellen? I don't understand," I said.

She blurted out that when the diagnosis came in he refused to let her go back to the doctor. "I knew what had to happen. When I met Henry I was in my final year of nurs-ing school. Never finished because he said that he wanted his wife at home. My father said that he didn't want to take care of another woman at home anymore. 'Women ain't worth much,' he'd tell me often, 'just to keep a house and keep a man happy.' If I didn't marry Henry, I'd have no home, no money, no life. We've been together now about ten years. No children. Days are long. Once I signed up for a community college course in anatomy, but Henry found out and had a fit. I hid the books and studied a bit on my own.

"Even before I went to the doctor I knew what the lump meant. When I finally went for the tests and got the results, it was clear—my only hope was surgery. I finally told Henry what I was going to do, and he got real mad." Now she looked down at her hands and continued, "He's my only family. I hope I'm doing the right thing."

I searched for words of hope and wisdom. I found none. I searched for words of comfort. I found none. Finally I blurted out words of outrage: "Henry is horribly wrong. Don't lis-ten to someone who would rather you die than have a breast removed. If he is that selfish he does not deserve you in his life." Now I was red-faced and furious. "How dare he ask you to die?" My ferociously gesticulating arms caused the vari-ous wires and tubes dangling from me to send out alerts, and nurses came quickly to settle me back into bed. Ellen and I talked into the night and when I awoke the next morning she was already off to surgery.

Henry did not come back that day.

When they wheeled her into our room, I held her hand

as she dozed. The following day I was sent home. I called her each day she was in the hospital. Henry never returned.

She told me she had a plan and assured me she'd be fine. "I'm determined to persevere," she told me the last time we spoke.

Three years later in 1979 I was back in Easton Memorial—this time for a full hysterectomy. There was no hope. My disease was too massive and uncontrollable. Surgery morning I was given medication and sent into a fitful slumber as I was moved onto the gurney. In the haze I felt a familiar hand take mine—and then darkness. Afterward the waking was difficult but I heard my name over and over and felt that hand in mine again.

Much later, back in my room, as nurses adjusted and arranged my bed around me, I saw a familiar face. It was Ellen. She smiled. I tried to speak: "Ellen. I never expected to see you again," I eked out. "What are you doing here?"

"I'm a nurse." She beamed. "I work on this floor—the Women's Floor. Henry left me and after the healing of my body and my heart, I decided that I was going to finish what I had started—I was going to get my nursing degree. It took me a few more years but here I am."

She smiled gently and continued. "See, when I saw how angry you were about how I was being treated I began to understand how much we all need each other. I don't mean just for everyday things, but for support—for caring. You didn't even know me but it made you so angry to see how my husband was with me. I don't want others to feel alone and scared. So I came back here to care for as many as I can."

I was beginning to nod off. She patted my hand and left. Later when I was woken up for my medication the night nurse told me that Ellen had been in to check on me a few times. "Darnedest thing too," she said, "it was her first day off in a long time, but here she was. Said you helped her a while back. She's the best nurse here—cares for everyone like they were her family."

CHAPTER 48

A STUDENT STORY: GRACE

"This rose tattoo (she pointed to her left arm) is in memory of my aunt. She raised me when my mom died. We didn't have much but she wanted me to have the best chance possible to do what I wanted to do—what I always felt I should do—be a nurse," Grace told me.

She came to my office on an early May day in 2004 as I was finishing grading the last of that semester's papers. I hadn't seen her since she was in my Introduction to Children's Literature class several years earlier. She sat down and continued, "When I started at the college I was scared a lot of the time. But my aunt reminded me to be strong." She lowered her head for a moment, then went on. "After she died I didn't think I could ever finish. I stopped going to classes and took small jobs where I could. I had no money. No hope. I was broken."

She continued, "One day when I was sleeping in my car in the college parking lot you knocked on my window to see if I was OK. You didn't even know me, but you wanted to see if I was OK."

Ah, yes, I remembered that cold December day—the dark gray clouds threatening snow, the wind seeping its way into any available crevice, and the young woman in her car with thin plastic covering a back window and thick tape attaching a door handle.

Grace continued, "I asked around later and found out who you were. That day I signed up for your class."

I smiled and said, "And I was so happy you did because I just loved reading your work. Such interesting perspectives on the fairy tales! And that essay you wrote about *Charlotte's Web* had me in tears—how you described the web of friendships and support was so moving."

She smiled almost shyly and said, "Do you remember what you told me after the first week when I said it was too much and that I'd never be able to read everything? I was in despair." Without giving me time she continued, "You told me that all literature was about our human family and our earth and our universal interdependence. To look at each work not just for what I thought I should be understanding, but for what I really was understanding about life. One small piece at a time."

Grace stood up, hugged me, and continued, "That's why I'm here. I found strength because in all those readings I saw how people need each other and how the world needed me. Me!" And then, "I wanted to show you this." And she took a shiny silver pin out of her pocket. "I'm a nurse now." I beamed as she went on, "Sometimes I wonder what I'd be doing or where I would be if you hadn't knocked on my window that day. And it reminds me how I want to be that person that helps others get a better chance in life. At the pinning ceremony I dedicated the pin to my Aunt Rose, but in my mind, I thought of you too."

I was humbled. Such a small gesture on my part and such large ripples.

Three years later during one of the first tennis lessons of my life I fell on a hard court and landed with my full weight on my left elbow. I could not move and was in intense pain. An ambulance came and whisked me away to the nearest emergency room. It was jammed with patients and I was placed on a gurney in the hallway. I could see people rushing by me—blurs of colors. Noises drifted cloudlike through my head as I struggled with consciousness. From what seemed like far away I heard a familiar voice give direct and authoritative instructions. It was calming. Someone was in charge. Someone was there to take care of each one of us in this swirl of seeming chaos.

And then, there she was, Grace, looking down at me. "Dr. Baer. Dr. Baer. It's me. We'll take good care of you. Your vitals are good. We have a few other patients before you, but we'll make sure you're fine. We can do this together."

She patted my foot and rushed off calling out instructions.

Minutes later there were X-rays and doctors and a dislocated, shattered left elbow. Most of it was hazy with intermittent darkness. "In shock," they told me. When I was discharged, Grace was there with all of the very specific instructions. She explained the next steps—preparation for surgery the following week—carefully and with gentleness. Her voice and her manner immediately created a sense of order and competence.

My worried husband thanked her for being so capable and for being so caring to each person amid such an intense crowd of patients. She bent down to my wheelchair level, looked straight into my eyes, and said: "I learned from the best." We both smiled.

And now it's January 2022 and Grace is in a major Philadelphia hospital caring for the unprecedented crush of patients. She wrote to me just a few days ago to tell me of a promotion. "It's hard work, but I feel like if I can make a difference in at least a few lives—help make their lives better—then it's all worthwhile. How are you doing, Dr. Baer?"

And I began my response to her, "It is my privilege and delight to begin the second semester of my 50th year of teaching . . ."

CHAPTER 49

NOTES

"I t's time," he said. "I've had it long enough." It was June 1977, I was twenty-seven years old and visiting my parents for a week from my new home in Maryland. My father motioned to his trumpet case sitting in the middle of our living room floor. "I turned fifty this week, and I haven't played in years." He was right. In truth, I only had very vague memories from when I was a young kid of him raising the trumpet up to his lips and holding it skyward as his fingers pressed keys and loud jazz music came tumbling out. The sounds seemed to enclose me and at the same moment make me feel giddily free.

In high school and college during the 1940s he had played in bands, mainly dance bands, and then for a few years was the leader of two of them. He played off and on since then, but by 1977 it had been many years. "It needs to be heard," he said to me with a soft sigh, and then continued, "The instrument isn't meant to sit in a closet idle—it needs to be shined up and be taken care of and make sounds. It was created to make music, not live in darkness."

That evening a local man came to the door. My father opened it and handed him the instrument case. The man, frayed hat in his shaking hands and a bit of cracking in his voice, thanked him. "Glad to do it!" my dad said, bowing his head slightly in recognition of the humanity between them. The man left, my dad stood looking at the closed door briefly, and then turned to walk back to where I was sitting.

I became sentimental. "Daddy, how can you just do that? How can you gladly give away something that valuable to you? You just gave it away."

"Well," he began, "I guess it depends on what you call 'valuable.' See, I love music. Love it with all my heart, but that trumpet sitting in a case isn't music. It needs to do what it was meant to do—make music. That's when it becomes gold."

More than twenty years later, I fully understood. I learned that the man who had come to the house had a teenage son who loved playing but the family could not afford a trumpet so he borrowed one whenever he could. My dad heard about him from a friend, called him up, and offered his trumpet. His father came to pick it up. Once the boy had my dad's trumpet in his hands, and realized it was fully his own, he hardly let it go—took it with him everywhere. It helped him get a scholarship to college which gave him openings into a career he dearly loved.

I learned this in 1999, just after my father died, when I

got a long condolence letter with an enclosed photo from the boy—now man—my dad had given the trumpet to. He wrote of how that simple gesture taught him a lot about life and people and the meaning of generosity. "It really comes down to being willing to give parts of yourself to others—Your dad gave me several gifts—the gift of his musical legacy, the gift of knowing I could create my own music whenever I wanted, and the gift of human kindness that has no limits of any type. I want you to know it does not stop with me. See, my son Jason is next."

The photo: A young boy—maybe nine or ten—holding a gleaming, giant-seeming golden trumpet in his small hands, grinning widely, with my dad's beaten-up instrument case proudly set up right beside him.

FRED KUHNER
CONCERTS, CARISSIMA, AND CLOSE ORDER DRILL

CHAPTER 50

ROADS

"I don't think I can finish this. It's too much—too many pieces. I don't think I can do it."

It had been a tough road for me as it is for all graduate students, but in 1986 I was almost finished with my PhD. Now, with a gulp of despair, I slumped into our living room couch. My husband listened as I questioned everything about what I was devoting so much energy to. I was tired. I was anxious. I was disillusioned.

"Look," he said, "we're going over to my dad's house for dinner tonight. You always like seeing him." He was right. His dad was a positive and energetic man who at almost ninety was working on community projects and traveling, and whose laughter filled the entire house with happiness.

That evening I told him, somewhat halfheartedly, that I was now beginning my dissertation—that this was the final piece. Pappa (as we called him) was a real cheerleader for me and took great pride in looking forward to having the first "Dr. Baer" in the family. A very intelligent man, he had had to put aside his young dreams of becoming a medical doctor when called home from college to run his family's farm. Without his managerial help, the banks told him, the farm would be lost. So, home he came to his Mennonite family where he built up the farm to eventually become a very thriving and successful business that supported his seven siblings and their children. He made sure all who wanted to, went to college. No one ever heard him complain. Once, when I asked him how he was able to do all of this, he just shook his head and tapped the side of the chair. "One (tap), step (tap) at a time (tap). You just do what you can and keep building on it. Gotta just stay with it."

He greeted my final step in the process with glee. "Oh, that's won'erful, won'erful, Sylvia," he gushed in his unique Maryland accent and took both my hands in his. "I want to give you a present. Something really special for when you graduate. What do you think you might want?"

This was an easy question for me to answer. I had always wanted a handmade quilt and I had recently seen a beautiful display of them created by local Mennonite women. The blending of disparate fabrics into specific, calculated, and yet initially seemingly random forms delighted me. I had tried to create smaller versions, but my hands were not meant for that sort of work. My small pillow coverings or baby quilts were quite serviceable, but my hands lacked true artistry. They were meant for other things.

And so he connected me to a distant relative of his—an older Mennonite woman who lived on a dairy farm just outside of our town in Western Maryland. When I met her a week later, Sara was dressed in her traditional long soft blue dress with her silver hair in what I learned was a "covering"—a white cap. Her blue eyes shining with possibilities and her soft pale skin folded like layers of gentle fabric on her face, she guided me in the process of creating. "First you look around the store and see what catches your eye. Then you keep looking and add more fabrics—might be the same color, might be totally different. Keep picking out fabrics that you like, and you'll see how it can all work together. You'll see. They all might look different, but the stitching'll make them work together."

I followed her instructions and came back to her two days later. "Oh, Sara, I had so much fun at the store," I gushed as I spread the blue, yellow, pink, and cream fabrics on her large kitchen table.

We sat in her front parlor where we looked at pictures of patterns. "Here's a log cabin one—see the rectangular pieces building it? And there's the rose of Sharon, and the Dresden plate, and the flying geese . . ."

"There it is," I said, leaping up. "It's perfect!" The pattern of overlapping circles of multicolored fabric pieces stitched together and then formed into one large bordered pattern delighted me immediately.

Sara smiled. "It's called the double wedding ring. Well, I best get started and you best be getting back to your own hand work."

Over the next several months as I worked through my writing, she worked on my quilt. Once a week I'd stop for a visit with her and watch as she guided her needle up and through layers of fabric held taut by the large quilting frame. We would chat pleasantly for a short while and then, refreshed, I would go back to my own work. Toward the end of my process I became increasingly frustrated that I couldn't quite make my chapters mesh together. All of my ideas seemed to be in myriad pieces around me and I felt despair at ever having them work together. On one such day I visited her and told her my dilemma.

She nodded her head gently and with understanding said: "You remember that pile of fabric pieces I had over there?" She motioned toward a large basket on her left. "Well, now look here," she said, pointing to the almost finished quilt. "See, it's not finished yet and if we just look at the top it doesn't look like much has happened. But you've got to look at the whole thing. Step back. Look. Remember where we started. Not finished yet, but just a little more and it'll be a beauty." I hugged her and rushed home.

A few weeks later I was done. Dissertation accepted and graduation in the very near future. I went to Sara's home to share the news. "Look," I squealed delightedly, "it's finished and approved! I'm done!"

"Well, you look here," she said with a smile as she handed me a big bundle wrapped in a white sheet. "This belongs to you now." And there it was: my beautiful quilt. She continued, "But I guess it's not really finished."

"I don't understand," I sputtered. "It's beautiful and exactly what we'd planned and worked for."

"No, you see, the quilt's not finished until it makes you calm and happy every day. And that takes a whole lifetime. And your work, your degree, isn't finished until you use it to help people learn and grow and help make the world better."

She was right. On both counts.

Her final words to me as I left her parlor, her house, her farm that day, still ring true: "All of us, we're just little tiny pieces in this world. But if we find ways to stitch ourselves together—to hold together—all of mankind can build a pattern." And she continued with a smile as she held the front door open for me to leave, "I would call that giant, beautiful pattern Peace."

CHAPTER 51

RELATED

I really didn't know how I'd react, and I was dreading it.

It was August 1990, I was forty years old, and my father's German Lutheran cousins were visiting the U.S. for the first time. My mother warned me in advance: "They were both members of Hitler's Youth in the 1930s. Nazis. I can't believe I will have them in my own home."

My father had tried to temper the situation. "Look, things are never that simple. They were very young. There must be a good explanation. After all, they seem like very kind people."

This did not placate my mother and she answered, "I'm only doing this because I love you and I know it's important to you, but if they say just one thing about Jews . . . just one . . . I'm leaving the house."

My father picked them up at the airport and on their way to my parents' home where my mother waited, they made a stop at mine. It was all very cordial and a bit stiff as I served tea and some small pastries in our living room. Small talk of the weather and the journey. Their English was very good.

And then it happened.

"Vas is this?" Wilma asked, smiling, as she pointed to a photo on my mantel.

I looked at my father and then back into her kindly blue eyes and answered, "That is my grandmother and all of her brothers and sisters. She's the oldest. This was taken around 1917 in Poland where they lived." Wilma's eyes widened. Henrik looked down. I continued, "Most of them along with their children died in concentration camps in the war." I sighed, unsure of where to look or what else to say or do.

Wilma spoke in a shaky voice: "It was a horrible time. Horrible."

I saw Henrik take her hand softly. He said, "We were children in 1933 when Hitler came to be so powerful. Men came to our school to tell us to sign up for youth programs. It seemed like a club to us. Nothing more. Nothing more." Now I began to see the interweaving complexities here. I nodded.

Wilma continued, "I was so angry one day. I was maybe seven or eight years old and men came to our school and took away books from our classrooms. I had a favorite book in my hand and they took it and said it contained poison ideas. I tried to grab it back and said it was only about a kitten. The men laughed at me and escorted me to the head of the school. I was punished for my actions but I didn't know why."

She stopped and looked again at the photograph and continued, "When I got home my mother was crying. She had been told of my defiance. 'Wilma, do not go against authorities anymore. Do as you are told. Don't speak out ideas. It is dangerous.' My father had just walked into the room and said, 'I don't recognize our country anymore. Our neighbors are being dragged from their homes. There is much hate and fear. I am afraid too for our family. Please, Liebchen, don't say anything more at school. Just follow orders.' I was very confused but my parents seemed scared. I had never seen them scared before."

Now Henrik spoke up: "I came home one day and found that my neighbor had disappeared. My mother was in ill health and fainted in front of me. I got water to help her and when she was conscious all she kept repeating was, 'Do what they say. Do what they say or they will kill you.'" He sighed.

My father poured more tea into all of our cups. Wilma continued, "It was only after the war that we learned the full details of the terror and atrocities." She sighed deeply and looked down.

I nodded and asked—by now genuinely interested in their stories—"How did your family fare during the war?"

Wilma looked at Henrik and then back at me and said, "My older cousin could no longer stand what was happening and he joined the resistance movement. He was killed in 1939. His mother died of grief a few months later. His children lived with my aunt in her attic until the war's end."

And then Wilma's eye caught a hat I had displayed on a table nearby. "What a beauty that is," she said softly.

I smiled and nodded and explained, "My grandmother made hats—she even had a successful store in Uruguay after she escaped from Poland." I got the hat and put it in Wilma's hands. She admired the artistry of it and softly stroked the velvety exterior.

"My mother loved hats too," she said. "She never made them, but she would embroider all of our clothes."

"Yes. My grandmother too loved to embroider. As do I!" I said, getting up and reaching for a nearby tablecloth. "Here, she made this," I said, handing her a richly stitched linen for her to admire. She ran her fingers along the patterns—her hands touching, in a way, my grandmother's.

Now it was getting late and my father was eager to get home.

With tears in his eyes Henrik hugged me goodbye. And then Wilma took both of my hands and held them for a long time as she said to me, "Please, Liebchen, you are teaching another generation. Help them to see the complexities of this world. And help them to see that what matters is love and peace. We are all human beings who are threads in this unimaginably big tapestry of the universe. Each thread matters to the final big picture. I'm so sorry for the loss of your family and for the pain."

I hugged her and said, "And I too am sorry for your loss and pain."

I called my mother right after they left. "Mom, they're on their way and Dad is right. It's very complicated. Listen to their stories. We need to listen to one another. We all need to learn."

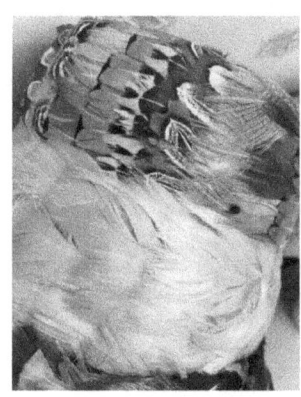

CHAPTER 52

A STUDENT STORY: ALISON

It was February 2006 when Alison jumped up out of her seat and quickly left the college seminar-type class I was teaching. The room was suddenly silent as the students stared at the now closed wooden door. We had been discussing the characters in Shakespeare's *Hamlet*. "I think Hamlet is just a whining fool," Jeff began earlier. "He's contemplating suicide because of circumstances around his father's death. Seriously? Just talk about it with others, dude." Rob jumped in, "Well, it was more complicated than that. He thought his father was murdered by his uncle and his mother might have been in on it. I mean, she got married to the guy really soon after Hamlet's father died. It was suspicious. I think Hamlet was just so totally overwhelmed by the enormity of it all that he couldn't see any way out of the pain." Sara joined in, "And he never does kill himself, does he? I mean he dies in the end,

but that's in a duel which is, theoretically, way more noble."
"Noble?" Carla chimed in. "I don't think any kind of killing
is noble. I mean if you kill someone to avenge the murder of
someone else, how are you any better? Any more noble?"

And so the discussion continued for several more lively
minutes—until the normally very quiet Alison spoke up.
"What about Ophelia? We're not even talking about her.
She drowns. We think it's a suicide. What about her?" There
seemed to be a desperation in her voice as she continued.
"There she is stuck in a horrible situation between Hamlet
who she loves and her own father and brother. She feels like
no one is on her side and they're all telling her what to do.
She is so confused and ends up lying for them and betray-
ing the man she loves." She looked at the ceiling, attempting,
it appeared, to hold back tears. "It made her go mad. She
lost all reason. Her head got so tangled up that nothing made
sense." And then, right before running out of the classroom:
"Sometimes even if you do everything you can, it still doesn't
help."

I asked the class to reflect on the character of the queen
and write down some ideas, and I then followed Alison down
the hall. She was sitting on a bench near the stairway, sobbing.
I sat next to her. "My sister," she began, "I tried to do everything I could. I talked to her. I begged her to go to therapy. I
think she went once and stopped. It was like her mind spun
spider webs and strange thoughts would get all caught up. She
couldn't get free of it. One day last year, April twenty-second,
I came home from school and the ambulance was there. They
did what they could, but she had been dead for a while before

my mom found her on the floor of the bathroom. They said it was pills. It was deliberate—a suicide." We both looked down at the floor. She took a deep breath.

"It seems to me," she began again, "that Hamlet had choices. He thought about things and somehow managed to cut through the pain. But Ophelia, well, she was so trapped by her circumstances, wasn't she? And then by her mind. And I think about this and I can see that both had so much agony, but they made such different decisions." Now Alison turned to look at me directly, her red, tear-filled eyes punctuating her words. "Life makes no sense sometimes. I wonder what it is that makes me not feel the way my sister did or the way Ophelia did. I feel pain. I feel anguish. I feel confused—even hopeless sometimes. But I wouldn't take the actions that they did. I just wouldn't. But I don't know what I'm supposed to do. Why am I so different than they were?"

I measured my own words very carefully. "Maybe," I began, "you're Horatio-like. He was always such a solid and good and reasonable friend to Hamlet. He tried however he could to help him. Still, there was only just so much he could do—Hamlet dies. But in the end, Horatio knew that his larger role was to be the teller of the tale—actually, Hamlet knew this and was comforted by it and even tells him so in his dying words." I heard Alison sigh gently, and then I continued, "Maybe you're meant to look at the world and be a guide of sorts. And a friend. And maybe your path is to, like Horatio does at the end, tell the story to others and hope you can help them somehow."

She brightened up. "Yes. That makes sense to me. Yes."

She went to the bathroom to wash her face and I returned to the class. When she came back into the room a few minutes later, Juanita and Jeremy were loudly debating whether wars were necessary or not, while several others were ready with quotes from Shakespeare to back up one of the two sides. Alison slid into her seat quietly, opened her book, and smiled up at me.

Today, fifteen years later, Alison is a counselor for troubled youths in a small city in the South. When she sends me emails or notes she always signs them "Horatio."

CHAPTER 53

THE WORLD'S FAIR

"Well, it didn't really go the way he planned."

It was 1999 and my father and I were waiting anxiously for his lab results from the hospital. I was sorting through some boxes of old postcards and pictures we had found in his cramped office closet. There was one of him standing in front of a strange contraption which I asked about.

"Oh," he continued, "I was almost twelve years old and my dad really wanted to encourage me to see science and engineering differently. He wanted me to follow in his footsteps. I just wasn't interested. So I guess he thought maybe going to the World's Fair in New York might encourage me. Because he helped to design some of the machinery, we got to go on opening day in April of 1939. 'Dawn of a New Day' was the slogan and I was keen to see what was there for the future. That picture is of a time capsule."

"A time capsule?" I asked.

"Yes," he continued, "it was buried and not to be unearthed for thousands of years, but they had a replica of all the things represented—books and music and art and science and even a cartoon of Mickey Mouse was there," he chuckled. "It was all in a small sort of cylinder and my father tried to explain how they compacted the information, but I was impatient and not interested. I wanted to see the pavilions of all the different countries I'd heard of. I went off by myself and just marveled at the number of cultures and their products—their materials and goods. The world is so vast and so full of interesting people and things. Every single one is so different—and yet we're all so connected. That variety makes the world one. I spent hours and hours."

I laughed imagining him as a kid wandering around looking and listening and taking it all in. He continued, "By the time of the 1964 World's Fair that you and I went to, a lot had changed. 'Peace and Unity' was the big slogan."

I laughed again and said, "As I recall, you were really interested in the countries then also. Even though I was only fourteen, I went off on my own because you just kept going back to the same places over and over."

He nodded in agreement and went on, "By then they had even more things and foods and I think I ate my way through the whole world." We dissolved into giggles.

"Remember how many times we went?" I asked.

"No," he answered, "too many to count. It was so close to where we lived then—took just minutes to get there. Every time someone came to visit we went again."

I remembered. The science exhibits intrigued me. So many things in communications (phones where you could see each other!), math (computer systems), transportation (new cars—Ford Mustangs), and energy. There were explosions of color everywhere and thousands of people to watch. But I was fascinated by the sounds of people most of all—the regional and international accents delighted me. I would listen for hours on end to people talking behind me in a tram car, or in front of me on a line, or around me as I sat on benches. Sometimes I would take out my little pocket notebook and write down phrases I overheard. Language filled my ears and pages.

"I remember thinking," he continued, "that going there might spark an interest in you in international business."

I smirked and answered, "You mean like you, Daddy? Well, that did not work out, did it?"

He chuckled: "No it did not. Do you remember the time you and your grandfather went off by yourselves? I don't think I ever asked you about that."

I remembered well. My father's father and I, growing weary of the hot June sun, cooled off in the Westinghouse pavilion. We sat talking about the machinery in there. I had a lot of questions. He had answers. Then we wandered around outside and ended up by the Unisphere—the gleaming, giant twelve-story structure at the center of the fair—a replica of the earth. He explained, "That is a monument to the globe and to the designers and builders who created it. See how it's balanced? Look, the winds have to blow through it and not knock it down. Time has to press against it, but it has to resist decay from corrosion and rust. So, they made it out of stainless steel and grit and promise and dreams and imagination." We both looked at it for a long time.

"Do you think it'll last forever, Grandpa?" I asked.

He didn't answer but led me over first to Michelangelo's *Pieta* sculpture and then to an ancient Roman column—both of which were carefully guarded and protected. "What lasts, Sylvia," he said, "is what is held dear. What is beautiful—so beautiful that people are willing to die to preserve it."

"Like sculpture? Art? Is that what you mean?" I asked.

He responded, "Not just that. Those represent what I mean. The Unisphere also represents what I mean. The moving stairways represent what I mean. Even the great earth itself represents what I mean." I looked at him as he spread his arms wide and continued with an intensity I had never seen in him before, "This ingenious collection of differences and of free ideas and creativity is what I mean. The human mind, Sylvia, and its constant energy toward progress—toward making things better. That freedom of the spirit all over the world in all manner of circumstances is what I mean."

Overwhelmed by the power of his words, I took out my notebook to write down what he said and he looked puzzled. I explained, "Sometimes I think that the whole world is like one giant story. I just write down some parts of it, but it's all connected everywhere into one." He asked me to read some lines from it. Then, silently, he hugged me and we walked on. "Grandpa, I know you wanted Daddy to be an engineer. Were you really disappointed he didn't do that?"

"I think I was at first, but I soon realized he had to go his own way. We have so many possibilities and so many roads we can go down. He had his. Why do you ask, Sylvia?" he responded.

I said, "I know he wants me to go into business and Mom wants me to be a doctor or lawyer, but I want to be a teacher. And a writer. They don't like that."

"We have to be who we are. We cannot be anything else," he said as we wandered back to the center of the fairgrounds. "We can build on the past, like this entire fair. You know, it was created on the grounds of the 1939 World's Fair. And that was built from a field of ash heaps—dumps. And look at it. It's not an ash heap and it's not what it was twenty-five years ago. No. It's now something entirely different." Then he grabbed my shoulders and turned me to look him square in the face. His deep blue eyes reflecting the brilliant sun, he continued, "You can use the past as foundation, but you create your own future. The force of your spirit will lead you there."

But now, in 1999, my father's future was limited. The phone rang, startling us both. The results came back from the hospital and they were not good. He and I sat amidst the photos and postcards from his past. Black and white and gray and sepia surrounding us. Neither one of us could talk. A picture slowly drifted off the couch like a feather in a soft wind—it was the one with him in front of the time capsule in 1939. He picked it up and spoke. "They buried another one in 1964, right in the same place. It'll be millennia before they unearth them. Imagine how different the world will be!" I tried to hold back tears. "You know, I think the life we each live are our individual time capsules—buried with us when we go." Now he took my shaking hand in his. "But we all leave pieces of ourselves behind as witnesses—representations of what was. Not the thing itself but standing in for it."

Now his steel-blue eyes met mine as he said, "That's our human spirit. It ties all of humanity together—the whole world—past, present, future. All. And it—the thing, the spirit, itself—cannot be buried."

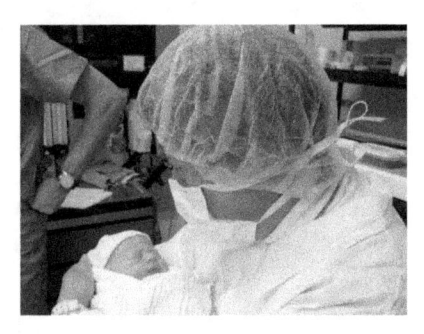

CHAPTER 54

THE PRESENT

I really had no idea what to expect. I knew there were no hidden jewels or objectively valuable pieces that she might have put in the safe-deposit box at our local small-town bank. And yet, my mother was very adamant about this: "If anything happens to me make sure you take everything in the bank box. I want you to have what's there. It's a present for you. It matters more than anything."

Just a month after my father's death in 1999, my mother began her litany: "Promise me you will go right away when I die. You will open the box right away. Promise me." Understandably, now alone, my mother was even more anxious than usual about everything. She had become severely handicapped and was beginning to suffer memory lapses and that, coupled with her sadness and anxiety, was almost too much for me to handle. Sometimes the stress of her seemingly end-less needs and demands drove me to tears.

"Mom. Stop talking about that box. Yes, I'll remember," I almost yelled one day in 2004 after spending another full day taking her to doctors' visits and testing, and then listening to her marathon harangue. "But you'll be fine, you're fine. You'll be alive a lot longer." She had heart problems. We all knew it. But she continually refused treatment. Pills were fine but nothing else. Sometimes my frustration spilled over into my voice. "You'll be fine, but there are things the doctors can do to really help you," I said to her.

She looked at me. "I miss your father. I didn't think he would ever die. But he did. And now here I am. I never under-stood . . ." And her voice trailed off as she stared out of the early August evening. So I took her small, cold hand and reassured her that I would, indeed, remember the box. She smiled.

The following week ambulances were called. "Massive blockages," the doctors said, "surgery needs to be done soon."

"I didn't realize I was so sick," she said to me in the intensive care unit of Cooper Hospital. The night before the surgery she reminded me yet again about the box. "Nothing is more important than what's in there."

She died during the triple bypass surgery.

The tragedy of life seemed to consume me for a while. I spent days just wandering about lost in a haze of grief and a queasy, strange emptiness. At fifty-four years old I suddenly felt myself to be an orphan. It wasn't until a few months later, when some balance came back to life for me, my husband,

and our daughter, that I remembered the box. What could be in there, I wondered as I waited for the official to bring it to me in one of the little, private cubicles the bank had created. After she left me alone, I opened it.

There, inside, was a tangle of watches. Old watches. New watches. Watches? I took one in my hand, an inexpensive Timex—one I had seen her wear many times—and gently wound it. I loudly gasped as the ticking started and I stared as the second hand made its round. A knock on the cubicle door: "Are you alright in there? Everything OK?"

"Yes," I exclaimed as I breathlessly swung open the door.

The official discreetly glanced down at the contents and smiled and said, "She used to come in pretty often after your dad died. She would go in there, stay a while, and always say to me that one day 'my daughter will be in for this box. She'll know just what to do with it.'"

Yes. I understood.

Her final precious gift to me was the same as her very first: Time.

CHAPTER 55

BEING

"You're not supposed to be in here, you know," he said in a firm but kind voice.

It was 1991, I was forty-one years old, and a participant in my first serious poetry workshop which was several days long and held at Mount Holyoke College in western Massachusetts. It was not far from where I'd spent four years at boarding prep school, so I was familiar with the region but had never seen it in its full summer glory.

I had just arrived and, having an hour before the first session, I wandered into the greenhouse, which is part of the botanical garden on campus. "I'm sorry. I guess I didn't realize . . ." I began, "but it looks so beautiful that I just couldn't seem to resist."

He smiled. "Name's Jim, I'm in charge here. And you are?"

I laughed and introduced myself and continued, "I think I'm sort of nervous about this whole event—not sure what to expect—and words are so important to me that I don't want to mess anything up. Being around plants of all kinds seems to calm me down."

His smile was broad and welcoming. "Well, I suppose it's OK for you to come in here. Just be real careful, right?"

I assured him I would and ran off ready and eager for the growth I was sure my first session would provide.

The following afternoon he found me slumped against a brick support half-wall, leaning on the back glass-domed structure, crying. "Hey, it's Sylvia, right?" he said, walking over to me. When he looked at my face he stopped, rather awkwardly looked away, and continued, "You need something? Someone I can get for you?"

Overwhelmed, I looked up at him and it all came blurting out like a waterfall or volcano. "I have no business being here at all. We have session after session of reading each other's poems and then critiquing them. Then our various leaders, all of whom are really esteemed poets, also critique our work. They tell us it's to help us improve. But I think I'm just about as hopeless as you can get. Other people's work always sounds more like what our instructors want. But everything I write seems like it's the wrong style or idea or image. There is no hope for me as a poet or writer anymore."

Jim handed me a crisp white handkerchief from his pocket. I wiped my eyes and managed a wan, grateful smile. "Well," he began, "I don't know much about poetry. Truth is

I don't know anything about poetry at all—never really cared for most of it myself." We both chuckled and he continued, "But I know a lot about plants. I can tell you that the Western Sword Fern is lush and bright green and loves cool shady spots. And the Autumn Fern lights up all shiny and brilliant gold in the spring before it turns to a duller green. Or that the Japanese Painted Fern looks like someone just brush-colored the edges of every single frond."

He smiled and ran his hand along the edge of a plant near us. "Or this," he said, "a Boston Fern that everyone seems to love and have in their homes." He continued, "I can tell you all about them, and how the plants all need different foods or soils. Each is an individual. And how they thrive in this greenhouse all winter because we keep the temperature at the right spots and the light can come in through all of these windows. We make this happen." As he spread his arm out in a gesture showing the expanse of this plant world, I saw the calluses on his palm and the dirt caked into his fingers

He continued, "It's all made possible because of this structure. But this structure needs to be repaired. After all of these years it needs to undergo a complete renovation. The metal skeleton needs tightening up, the glass needs to be replaced in lots of spots and tightened in, the irrigation system needs to be brought up to date. It all needs a sort of . . ." He couldn't find the word.

"Reinvigorating," I volunteered.

"Yes," he bellowed, "that's the exact word!"

I was puzzled why he was telling me all of this, but

delighted to be hearing this story. He continued, "So you see, I think that maybe lots of systems and programs and ideas and even things like poetry have structures that need"—he smiled and winked—"reinvigorating. They work well for a while, but then need updating or changing. We grow these plants in here to show folks all about them, but they grow best out there in their own world. We provide some plants a safe place—a structure—for a while. But then all sorts of plants— they all thrive in different environments."

I nodded with the start of an understanding spreading across my mind. I wanted to hug him, but Jim didn't seem the sort, so I smiled and thanked him as I almost bounced out of the decaying greenhouse into the warm late afternoon sunshine.

The next day's workshops were just as difficult as the first ones, but I was more vocal. I asked "why" about a lot more and began to see that what was being provided for me was simply a space to grow. But the environment of that specific workshop was just that—one environment.

That afternoon I found myself in the large grassy amphitheater at the edge of campus and looked out at the trees, the peonies, the budding roses, around me. "In my own way, I'm going to be a poet," I wrote in my notebook, musing in a stream of consciousness, and continued, "and the form I take or the style I take will be different. But poetry and writing are like a greenhouse that gives sheltering structure, but also needs to be reinvigorated. And maybe some plants grow best outside of it in whole new environments. Maybe this is true for a lot of other things . . ."

I heard noises and I looked up to see Jim in the distance hauling some things in a wheelbarrow, bringing needed change and support to his world. I waved wildly and yelled a hearty "thank you" to him. He tipped his hat, raised his arm in greeting, and kept at his tasks.

Talcott Greenhouse

CHAPTER 56

STARSHINE

"Why are we dragging all of those toys up from the basement?" It was November 1996 and my husband, John, who by now was very used to my quirkiness, was helping me lug boxes of toy houses and farms and vehicles up the stairs and into our family room. I was forty-six years old and our daughter was away at her first semester of college and two months earlier we had tucked away her childhood items in boxes.

"Well, the Tanaka family is coming for dinner tomorrow and I want to have something for their little kids to do," I replied.

In truth, I was really grasping at straws.

The Tanakas were visiting from Japan. Mr. Tanaka, whom John had met twenty-five years earlier when he lived in Japan, was now a famous surgeon and had attended a conference in Philadelphia for the past week. His English was perfect. His wife, however, had tried to learn a bit of the language before this trip (her first trip abroad) but her communication was spotty. And since the kids, four and five years old, spoke no English at all, they spent most of their time in the hotel. Mr. Tanaka insisted on it. The conference was over and in a few days they were heading back to Tokyo.

I had never met any of them, did not speak Japanese, and was a bit apprehensive. So I was trying to find all manner of ways to make them comfortable in my home.

Dinner was a blur. John reminisced with Mr. Tanaka, but there were lulls in the conversation. The kids finished eating quickly and were eager to play with the toys. Mrs. Tanaka, Akari, smiled at me throughout the meal, but we did not speak.

After the main course, I stood up to clear the table and she stood up with me. "I help," she said, gathering up the dishes. I smiled. Once in the kitchen she pointed to my plates and said, "Beautiful. Where from?"

Oh, she liked my cherished dinnerware! I turned it over to show her the stamp on the back, and said, "Wedgewood. Very old."

She giggled delightedly. "Me," she said, pointing to herself, "I love Wedgewood. I have some." And, pointing to my dress, she said, "Laura Ashley?"

Now I giggled. "Yes," I responded, "it's new," and I twirled around in my pink-blossom-filled flowing dress.

She pointed to an embroidered sampler on my wall and asked me something in Japanese which somehow I understood.

"Yes. Me," I said, pointing to myself, "I did that." And then she looked at my hair.

"Beautiful cut," she said admiringly. And then slumped into a chair and pulled at her own hair. "No beautiful," she said sadly.

In this fashion we chatted amiably as we gathered dessert and took it into the dining room. "We've hatched a plan," I exclaimed. "Akari and I are taking the train into New York tomorrow. She's never been."

Now Akari chimed in. "New York cut," she said, smiling and holding out a lock of her hair. Her husband seemed very angry and began a tirade in Japanese. I looked at John, who quietly interpreted that Mr. Tanaka was upset that he would have to watch the kids all day. Akari's head bowed down.

I chimed in, "I will pick her up at the hotel tomorrow at 9 AM. I will bring toys for the children to play with."

She looked up. "New York cut," and smiled at me.

Akari and I spent a glorious day in the city. We shopped and saw sights and ate and had tea and even found that one of the hairstylists at a famous department store hair salon was from Tokyo. As he snipped and styled, she chattered with him in Japanese about her home and about hair and about life. When she went to the register to pay, the stylist sighed. "Your friend is so lonely," he said. "She told me how in Tokyo she has no friends. Her husband won't allow any of them into the house. He says they're not good enough, and so she spends a lot of time alone."

Now Akari, her dark, chin-length hair bouncing and gleaming, came toward us. She twirled, struck a pose, and said, "New York cut beautiful. I beautiful." We clapped and cheered and left for home.

Next to each other on the train, she showed me some worn photos in her purse. "Mama," she said, pointing to an older woman in an apron, "live far from Tokyo. Sad." And to another photo, this time of her wedding day with her husband, where she pointed to herself and said, "Sad."

By the time we got off the train we were laughing like old buddies. The sky was particularly clear that night and our walk back to the hotel in the crisp November air was filled with promise. She stopped and looked up. Pointing toward the constellation near the horizon, she sputtered a word. I said, "Stars," but she said, "No, many stars." And I realized what we were looking at. "It's the Pleiades constellation," I said. "Sisters together. There were seven but one married a mortal and now they all take care of each other. Like good friends."

Akari sighed as we both looked at the glittering stars in their correct sky positions but moving imperceptibly even as we watched—gliding toward a new destination tiny bit by tiny bit. "In Japanese called Subaru," she said. And then she continued, "Means bring together."

We reached the hotel and went up to their room. Mr. Tanaka was taken aback by Akari's appearance. He clearly disapproved of her hair and her giddiness, and as I hugged her goodbye, she looked at me and then directly at his startled face as she said, "Sylvia is my friend."

Ten years later a mutual friend came to visit us from Japan. As he and John spoke of old times, I asked about Akari. "Oh my," he began, "now that was a scandal. Soon after she came back from her visit to the U.S. she took her two kids and moved back in with her parents. They're on an island far from Tokyo. Tanaka was fuming with rage. Made so many threats to her. But somehow, she stayed strong. We all knew how terribly he had treated her but never thought she'd have the strength to do anything about it. He died about five years ago. Heart attack."

"And what's Akari doing now?" I was eager to know.

"Well," our friend replied, "she opened up a salon and spa in her town. It's very successful. Women always love going there. But it has an odd name. She called it 'Subaru.'"

"Like the car?" my astonished husband asked.

I answered, smiling delightedly, "No, like the sister stars."

CHAPTER 57

SPACE

"Let's just think about this moment right now. I mean it's just breathtaking," he implored. It was July 20, 1969, I was nineteen years old and in our living room watching the first manned lunar landing with my boyfriend. "The Eagle has landed," we heard the astronaut say in mid-afternoon just as touchdown happened. We cheered and my parents rushed in the room from the kitchen to join in the celebration.

But no matter how hard I tried to be happy, I was haunted by confusion and sadness. There was so much anger and discord in the world that the very air we breathed seemed filled with frustration and anxiety. Just a few months earlier I had been in a civil rights peace march that had ended with several friends sent to jail and two others hospitalized.

And the prospect of a never-ending war in Vietnam meant that many of the guys I knew, including my boyfriend, were worrying about an upcoming draft. "I think they're going to do some sort of lottery system," I heard Jerry, my brilliant classmate, say just yesterday. "That means that all of our birthdays will be put in a container, like mine September 14th, and as they're randomly drawn out, that's the order that guys will be drafted," he explained.

And the country was so divided on this whole matter. People yelling back and forth to each other on streets and in buses and in churches and even, this summer, on the beach. "America, love it or leave it," screamed those in favor of shoring up the military by drafting. "Stop the immoral war," yelled those opposed. It went on and on and on.

I was in despair at anything ever being in balance again.

Because we had to wait a few hours for Neil Armstrong to actually step on the moon, we made dinner and listened to the radio. "Alien theories abound," we heard blasted out with eerie background music at the start of one show about green monsters being unleashed by disturbing the moon's surface.

It would have been comical except that the word "alien" reminded me of ten years earlier.

My dad and mom and I were in a post office in Passaic, NJ, in 1959 filling out some paperwork when nine-year-old me saw a giant poster on the wall imploring "All aliens must absolutely be registered here." "Who is an 'alien'?" I asked, thinking of Martians and space invader creatures from comic books. My dad patiently explained that my mom and I were in that category and that's why we were there. "Until you're citizens at the end of the year," he explained. He handed me my papers to give to the clerk.

"But I want to be clear," I explained to the bespectacled man who grinned kindly as I spoke, "that we're from Uruguay. And that country is far away, but we are not strange creatures. We're just people. You need to change that word 'alien' on your poster because it just makes us all sound too scary. And we're not." He nodded and smiled in understanding as my dad tipped his hat and took my hand to lead me out the big glass door.

And now, in 1969, with the air full of turbulence about immigrants, civil rights, war, and the future of the world, a man was going to step on the moon for the first time in history and we were all going to actually watch it and hear it as it happened.

But even in my awe at the enormity of this scientific accomplishment, I held back my joy. I barely touched my lasagna, a usually favorite dinner. "I'm having trouble with humanity," I finally stated.

My father chuckled. "All of it, or just certain parts?"

Now I was adamant. "I'm serious. People just can't seem to work together to make things happen other than wars. Why can't we do things that bring us harmony instead of all this tearing apart? We are all people and we all deserve dignity." In a symbol of disgust, I almost tossed down the fork I'd been dragging aimlessly around my plate. Tears were building up behind my eyes.

"Come with me," my dad stated with an uncharacteristically forceful voice as he plunked down his napkin. I followed him out of the room as my mother and boyfriend watched, stunned.

In the living room he pulled out a few history books and some magazines. For the next hour he showed me picture after picture of amazing structures all over the world. He showed me illustrations of horrible events that no longer happened because of changes in laws and policies. He showed me advances in science that had extended human life and reduced human suffering. "You see, Sylvia, yes, humans can be cruel and turn away from suffering. Yes, that is true. But look at all of the advances. Look how individuals can change just one thing and then it snowballs into greater changes."

Then he showed me a magazine spread of the mission control centers of NASA. "Do you see all of those people working together? Each individual has a part to play in making this lunar landing possible. It would not happen unless everyone worked together for just one rocket and just two men to step on the moon. And they did it for exactly this event, but also because this experience could lead us to new discoveries in the future. Maybe one day we'll have all sorts of satellites helping to guide us even in our everyday lives. Or maybe what we learn can help us communicate with better and faster systems. We can't even begin to imagine how what they did in this event can impact the world for the better in fifty or a hundred years from now."

I sighed. He was right. I had been so caught up in the fear and trepidation that permeated our newspapers and televisions. I had always believed that the good in the world far outweighed the bad, and for a brief moment I had forgotten.

At 10:39 PM Eastern Time, we watched as Neil Armstrong opened the hatch, stepped onto the surface of the moon, and uttered his famous words, "One small step for man—one giant leap for mankind." And then with the second astronaut, Buzz Aldrin, he left a plaque inscribed with "Here men from the planet Earth first set foot on the moon—July 1969 A.D.—We came in peace for all mankind." I was awestruck by this miraculous human endeavor and by the humbleness and bravery of these men sharing the stunning achievement with thousands of people who made it possible, and millions—billions—in the future, all of mankind, who this might in some unknown way benefit. And the mention—right there for all eternity—of peace.

I took a deep clear breath. The good in the world, I was once again convinced (and am convinced still, all these years and life later), will always soar to tower above all of life. The future, gladly and moonshiny and full of hope, beckons.

CHAPTER 58

BUILDING LIFE

"Abuela," I said, plunking my bag of books and papers on the nearby table, "I've decided. I am going to get a master's and maybe even a PhD in English. I'm going to study literature and read and write and teach for the rest of my life." It was 1974 and my grandmother was visiting my husband and me at our brand-new home in Maryland. I was twenty-four years old and teaching seventh grade which I loved, and I had been waffling about my future. "Papa wants me to go into business—says I have a head for it. He'll be disappointed."

As she did every afternoon while visiting, my abuela poured steaming hot coffee with a little milk and a lot of sugar into my favorite mug—the one with bright green vines encircling the rim and wrapping themselves around the handle. She put it down on the table next to my bag while I kicked off my shoes. The warmth of the liquid soothed my tired throat.

"Did I ever tell you about my father?" she began. I turned my head from side to side in a "no" and kept sipping. "He started a store in the downtown area of our town of Łomża in Poland—I think it was 1905—and he put a big sign out front with our last name: 'Jelin.' It was a haberdashery for men, but he sold some women's clothes as well. Not many, but in those days, it was mainly tailors. You would go to the store, pick out the fabric and the style, they would measure you, and then they'd make your clothes. It was an elegant place, and he was successful at every part of it. I was always well-dressed, and he would tell me I was a walking advertisement for his store."

I knew nothing about this. She continued, "But he didn't want me to have any part in it. 'It's not for women to do these things,' he'd say to me. 'Women should keep house and have children. That should be all.' And he'd shake his head. He was a good man, but I think I was a mystery to him. I was always thinking up ideas and plans and reading and having fun. 'You laugh too much, Malka,' he'd say, 'and you have too much silliness.' I was the oldest—there were thirteen of us—and supposed to be the most responsible."

Now she took a sip of her own coffee and looked out the big picture window at the suddenly darkening clouds. "I think he believed I did everything wrong—the sneaking off to university to get a degree, the marrying my first husband, the children we could not afford. But I left Poland early looking for possibilities. There had to be a better life somewhere else. I think when he started his store my father taught me that: look for possibilities. And I was one of the few of us who survived. Most of the others were killed in the camps and the pogroms.

"When I got to Uruguay with the two little ones and no husband, we moved right away into a place called Villa Muñoz. It was a small area of Montevideo where all the Jews lived—a tight-knit community there. How to feed the babies? Oy, I thought and figured and then I came up with the idea of a hat store. I knew fashion. I knew sewing. I knew what was elegant and what was fun. Everyone said it was impossible, but I did it. And I changed my name too. I wanted to be someone new. So I made Malka into Margot. Ah, so many possibilities with a French name like that!" And now she gave me a sly wink and we both doubled over with laughter.

"And you named it 'Casa de Margot,'" I said, "because I remember it clearly."

She smiled. "Oh, I was so proud to see that sign over the window. Like my father's store—but it was mine. With my name for all the world to see."

Loud claps of thunder startled us both. "I worked hard," she continued, "and every day brought new possibilities to me—even after my husband who deserted me showed up and stole everything, twice, before disappearing again. Even after your mother married her first husband, Harry, and he was so awful to her and then to you and then he, too, disappeared. My store—it had my name. It said to me that anything was within my power. It marked my place in the universe loud and clear."

The rain began pounding the windows sounding like pebbles crashing into glass. I shivered. She continued, "So you see, my dear granddaughter, what I want to tell you is that maybe your father has ideas for your life, or your mother, or your husband, or your friends, but they don't have to live it: you do. So you should do with your life what matters to you. What speaks to your heart. No one else's. Maybe you'll be rich. Maybe you'll be poor. But you will always get to be you. Build your own life of possibilities." I nodded, gratefully, feeling a surge of strength.

The rain had stopped and a small ray of sun shone through the clouds, making the grass, the leaves, the flowers sparkle like little jewels.

Two years later she died.

I did get a few master's degrees and my PhD. I have spent more than fifty years teaching and reading and studying and writing. And a few years ago I named a building of my own, my house at the beach in Cape May, where I hang poems on a tree and encourage passersby to take them—sort of selling, but for free, not clothing or hats but what I love, literature.

In a ceremony with my two grandsons I formally named it: Possibility Cottage.

ACKNOWLEDGMENTS

Thanks go to Marc J. Lane of the law offices of Marc J. Lane and Company for encouraging this project and for bringing me together with my wonderful (and patient) agent Tim Brandhorst without whom this book would never have been created. I thank him for his wisdom, guidance, and clarity.

Thanks also go to the many students and colleagues whose life-journeys I've been privileged to be part of for more than 50 years. You have enriched my life.

My friends, both near and far, and those introduced via the technological ether, I thank you for your kind and thoughtful readings of my work and for your friendship and support. It has emboldened me.

To my generations upon generations of family now gone from this earthly realm, I thank you for the sacrifices and bravery and love of life that have given me such a rich bank of stories and have given me existence.

To my extended family today, I thank you for your support and love which gives meaning to all I do. You will carry our shared stories forward.

To my daughter, Heather, and grandsons Miles and Jameson, all of whom bring the love of justice and caring into the world, I look forward to your future.

And, ultimately, to my husband John Baer, who has made our shared life better and richer and more glorious than any words could capture, I give my never-ending gratitude.

ABOUT THE AUTHOR

Sylvia Baer who is a teacher, poet, storyteller, and translator was born in Montevideo, Uruguay and has lived in many countries and speaks several languages. She has been teaching English Literature for over 50 years, has created creative writing programs and publications, and been the founding editor of several national academic journals. She has written and performed a one-woman play, "A Passion for Life" where she embodies the poet Emily Dickinson. She is a graduate of Northfield School (now NMH), Washington College (BA and MA) and The University of Maryland (PhD), an Associate Fellow of Yale University (Davenport), and was recently named the first Poet Laureate of Cape May, NJ, where you can visit her Poet-Tree and her free-to-the-artists art gallery, Art Space. Her book, *Learning Life: A Memoir*, Volume 1, was published in August of 2022. She is married to John Baer, has one daughter and two grandsons, and loves to play tennis and golf, gardening, and learning tap-dance and ballet.